Merry Christmas Sam!
12/25/15

SECRETS OF
UNIVERSAL
ORLANDO
REVEALED

TIPS AND FACTS
to Get the Most
Out of Your Visit

Love You!,
Mom & Dad :)

LAURIE FLANNERY

FALL RIVER PRESS

New York

FALL RIVER PRESS

New York

An Imprint of Sterling Publishing
1166 Avenue of the Americas
New York, NY 10036

Cover Design: David Ter-Avanesyan

Book Design: Michele L. Trombley

ISBN 978-1-4351-5911-2

Manufactured in China

2 4 6 8 10 9 7 5 3 1

www.sterlingpublishing.com

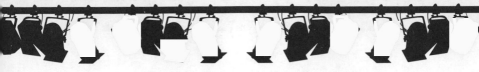

CONTENTS

RESORTS, ATTRACTIONS, DINING, SHOPPING, AND MORE . . .

To MAKE THE MOST OF your visit to Universal Orlando Resorts, use this handy list of rides, attractions, shopping, dining options, and amenities organized by resort and hotel.

Universal Studios Florida

Rides and Attractions

Animal Actors on Location!℠

Beetlejuice™ Graveyard Revue

The Blues Brothers Show®

Curious George® and Curious George Goes To Town℠

A Day in the Park with Barney™

Despicable Me Minion Mayhem

Disaster!℠ – A Major Motion Picture Ride...Starring YOU

E.T. Adventure®

Fear Factor Live

Fievel's Playland®

Hollywood Rip Ride Rockit®

Kang & Kodos' Twirl and Hurl

Lucy – A Tribute℠

MEN IN BLACK ™ Alien Attack ™

Revenge of the Mummy®

Shrek 4-D

The Simpsons Ride™

Terminator 2®: 3D

TRANSFORMERS™: The Ride-3D

TWISTER...Ride It Out®

Universal Orlando's Horror Make-up Show

Universal's Cinematic Spectacular: 100 Years of Movie Memories®

Universal's Superstar Parade®

Woody Woodpecker's KidZone

Woody Woodpecker's Nuthouse Coaster®

Dining

Ben and Jerry's

Beverly Hills Boulangerie

Bone Chillin' Beverages

Bumblebee Man's Taco Truck

Café La Bamba

Duff Brewery

Fast Food Boulevard:
  Cletus' Chicken Shack
  The Frying Dutchman
  Krusty Burger
  Lisa's Teahouse
  Luigi's Pizza

Finnegan's Bar and Grill

Kid Zone Pizza Company

Lard Lad Donuts

Lombard's Seafood Grille

Louie's Italian Restaurant

Mel's Drive-In

Moe's Tavern

Ritcher's Burger Co.

Schwab's Pharmacy

Starbucks®

Universal Studios' Classic Monsters Café

Shopping

Aftermath®

The Barney® Store

Brown Derby Hat Shop

Cyber Image

E.T.'s Toy Closet & Photo Spot®

It's a Wrap

Kwik-E-Mart

MIB Gear

On Location

Sahara Traders

San Francisco Candy Factory

Shrek's Ye Old Souvenir Shoppe

Silver Screen Collectibles

SpongeBob Store Pants™

Studio Sweets

Supper Silly Stuff

Supply Vault

Universal Studios Store®

The Wizarding World of Harry Potter

The Hogwarts™ Express
(Runs between Hogsmeade Station and King's Cross Station)

Hogsmeade™ (inside Universal's Islands of Adventure)

Attractions

Dragon Challenge™
Flight of the Hippogriff™
Gryffindor™
Harry Potter and the Forbidden Journey™

Dining

Hog's Head™
Three Broomsticks™

Shopping

Dervish and Banges™
Filch's Emporium™ of Confiscated Goods
Honeydukes™
Ollivanders™
Owl Post™

Diagon Alley™ (inside Universal Studios Florida)

Attractions

Gringotts™ Bank
Harry Potter and the Escape from Gringotts™

Dining

Eternelle's Elixir of Refreshment
Florean Fortescue's Ice-Cream Parlour
The Fountain of Fair Fortune
The Hopping Pot
Leaky Cauldron™

Shopping

Borgin and Burkes™
Madam Malkin's Robes for all Occasions
Magical Menagerie
Ollivanders™
Quality Quidditch™ Supplies
Scribbulus
Shutterbutton's™ Photography Studio
Wands by Gregorovitch
Weasley's Wizard Wheezes
Wiseacre's Wizarding Equipment

Universal's Islands of Adventure

Rides and Attractions

Amazing Adventures of Spider-Man®

Camp Jurassic®

Caro-Seuss-el™

The Cat in The Hat™

Dr. Doom® and Dr. Doom's Fearfall®

Dudley Do-Right's Ripsaw Falls®

The Eighth Voyage of Sinbad®
Stunt Show

High in the Sky Seuss Trolley Train Ride

If I Ran the Zoo™

The Incredible Hulk Coaster®

Jurassic Park and Jurassic Park Discovery
Center®

Jurassic Park River Adventure®

The Lost Continent

Marvel Super Hero Island

Me Ship, The Olive®

One Fish, Two Fish, Red Fish,
Blue Fish™

Popeye & Bluto's Bilge-Rat Barges®

Pteranodon Flyers®

Poseidon's Fury®

Seuss Landing

Sneetches™ and Sneetch Beach™

Storm Force Accelatron®

Toon Lagoon

Dining

Arctic Express

Blondie's: Home of the Dagwood

The Burger Digs®

Café 4

Captain America Diner®

Cathy's Ice Cream

Cinnabon®

Circus McGurkus Café Stoo-pendous™

Comic Strip Café®

Confisco Grille®

Croissant Moon Bakery®

Doc Sugrue's Desert Kebab House

Fire Eater's Grill

Green Eggs and Ham™ Café

Hop on Pop™ Ice Cream Shop

Moose Juice, Goose Juice

Mythos Restaurant®

Pizza Predattoria®

Thunder Falls Terrace®

The Watering Hole℠

Wimpy's

Shopping

All the Books You Can Read

Betty Boop Store

Cats, Hats & Things™

The Coin Mint

Comic Book Shop

DeFoto's Expedition Photography®

Dinostore ℠

Gasoline Alley

Historic Families –Heraldry

Islands of Adventure Trading Company

Island Market and Export® Candy Shoppe

Jurassic Outfitters®

Marvel Alterniverse Store®

Mulberry Street™ Store

Ocean Trader Market®

The Pearl Factory

Port of Entry Christmas Shoppe

Port Provisions®

Snookers & Snookers
  Sweet Candy Cookers

Spider-Man Shop

Star Souls-Psychic Reading

Toon Extra®

Treasures of Poseidon®

Universal CityWalk

AMC® Universal Cineplex 20 with
  IMAX®

Antojitos Authentic Mexican Food

Blue Man Group

Bob Marley—A Tribute to Freedom℠

Bread Box

Bubba Gump Shrimp Co.™

Burger King

Cinnabon

Citywalk's Rising Star

Cold Stone Creamery

The Cowfish™ Sushi Burger Bar

Element

Emeril's™ Restaurant Orlando

Fat Tuesday

Fresh Produce®

Fossil®

Fusion Bistro Sushi & Sake Bar

The groove℠

Hard Rock Cafe®

Hard Rock Live®

Hart & Huntington Tattoo Company®

Hollywood Drive-In Golf™

Hot Dog Hall of Fame®

The Island Clothing Company

Jimmy Buffett's™ Margaritaville®

Lone Palm Airport

Menchies

Moe's Southwest Grill

NBA City

Panda Express

Pat O'Brien's® and the Hurricane® drink

Quiet Flight® Surf Shop

Red Coconut Club®

Red Oven Pizza Bakery

Starbucks

Universal Studios Store®

Vivo Italian Kitchen

Hotels and Water Parks

Loews Royal Pacific Hotel

Bula Bar & Grille
Emeril's Tchoup Chop
Islands Dining Room
Jake's American Bar
Orchid Court Lounge
Orchid Court Sushi Bar
Wantilan Luau

Hard Rock Hotel

The Bar American
Beachclub
Bice Ristorante
Emack & Bolio's Marketplace
Gelateria
The Kitchen
Loews Portofino Bay Hotel
Mama Della's Ristorante
Mandara Spa
Palm Restaurant
Sal's Market Deli
Starbucks
Splendido Bar & Grill
The Thirsty Fish®
Trattoria del Porto®
Velvet Bar

Cabana Bay Beach Resort

Atomic Tonic
Bayliner Food Court
Starbucks
Swizzle

Wet 'n Wild Waterpark

Aqua Drag Racer™
The Black Hole™: The Next Generation
The Blast
Blastaway Beach™
Bomb Bay
Brain Wash™
Bubba's Fried Chicken
Der Stuka
Disco H2O™
The Flyer
Lazy River
Mach 5
Manny's Pizza & Subs
The Storm
Surf Lagoon
The Surge
Unlimited BBQ

INTRODUCTION

THE UNIVERSAL ORLANDO RESORT IS a multipark, multiresort entertainment destination, comparable in many ways to a nearby vacation resort that's run by a certain famous mouse. But Universal Orlando Resort has carved out its own niche, with high-tech cutting-edge thrill rides, more entertainment for adults to enjoy, and the addition of a wildly popular young wizard's world.

Here's a quick breakdown. Universal Orlando Resort consists of two amusement parks: Universal Studios Florida, including The Wizarding World of Harry Potter – Diagon Alley; and Universal's Islands of Adventure, including The Wizarding World of Harry Potter – Hogsmeade. There is also a nighttime entertainment complex called CityWalk (which is largely for adults) and four on-site hotels with a fifth scheduled to open in 2016. Neighboring Wet 'n Wild Waterpark is not officially part of the Universal Orlando Resort, but is owned by Universal and visitors can obtain special ticket packages that include a visit there.

If you compare the size of Universal Orlando's amusement parks to other well-known parks you'll immediately notice that Universal is smaller. But hold on: this doesn't mean there's less to do. In fact, these parks are designed to be more compact, with attractions within easy walking distance of each another. So, you'll get to enjoy many of these cool attractions in a shorter amount of time and with less walking. The theming details are still a big part of this resort's style even though it's more compact. In fact, The Wizarding World of Harry Potter has taken theming to a whole new level.

Both Universal Studios Florida and Islands of Adventure are jam-packed with fun for people of all ages. I've heard many visitors remark that these parks are for adults and older children only, but I disagree. Both parks have a themed land specifically for young children; there's plenty of magic to interest young kids in the Harry Potter lands as well as other areas throughout the parks. You may need to divide and conquer if you have a family with younger and older children, but these parks certainly offer something exciting for all ages.

Before we begin discussing everything you'll find at Universal Orlando Resort, the following section provides some insider's information to make the most of your overall experience. Visitors can save a great deal of time, and make their trip easier, by taking advantage of these tips.

Best Time to Ride an Attraction

Wait times for each attraction fluctuate throughout the day and depend on how busy the park is. Ask the ride attendant to suggest a good time to come back when the line won't be excessively long. There's no way to perfectly predict the best moment to ride, but oftentimes the folks who work at that attraction can make a fairly good estimate. Another very helpful tool is Universal's free app, which provides current wait times on attractions.

> *Note: Sometimes the wait time posted at an attraction is actually longer than it really is, so it's worth asking the attendant if the sign is accurate.*

Universal Express℠ Passes

Universal has a separate "express line" for most, but not all, of the attractions in its parks. This decreases your wait time significantly. Two types of Express Passes are available for purchase. The Universal Express Pass is for limited use, allowing the guest to access the express line one time per attraction in that single day. The Universal Express Unlimited Pass allows visitors to use the express line as many times as they wish, on each day the pass is valid. If you visit the parks on a busy day, the extra fee is well worth it.

There is also a two-park Universal Express Pass or Universal Express Unlimited Pass option for folks who are planning to see both parks in the same day.

Guests who stay at Universal's on-site hotels—with the exception of the value-priced Cabana Bay Beach Resort—receive a free Universal Express Unlimited Pass.

Note: Express Passes are not valid on the Hogwarts Express, Harry Potter and the Escape from Gringotts, Harry Potter and the Forbidden Journey, and other select attractions.

Single Rider Lines

One way to avoid long queues is to ask for the single rider line, which usually moves very quickly. Here are some more tips...

* Sometimes the single rider line is the same as the express line.
* When you reach the boarding area as a single rider, you are not allowed to board with a friend, but there are many times you'll end up together anyway due to the way the ride is boarded. (no guarantees)
* Not all attractions have a single rider line, and it is opened only at the discretion of the ride attendant.
* Sometimes the single rider line takes a shorter, different path, so you'll miss some interesting details within the attractions' regular queue.

Lockers

Several of the rides inside both parks are so physically intense that Universal does not allow you to carry any loose objects, including purses, backpacks, cameras, and sometimes even sunglasses and phones. To solve this problem, there are several well-placed free locker stations where you can store your items while riding. You won't even need a key to access that locker because it uses fingerprint technology.

Note: You can use the lockers for free for a limited period of time. If you want to use the locker all day, you'll pay a fee.

VIP Experience

Universal Orlando Resort offers a very special (though costly) VIP Experience for those who want to see the parks like a rock star.

The VIP Experience is a specially guided tour of the park and guaranties immediate access (through a back door) to at least eight attractions. (The guide will decide which attractions best fit the group.) In addition to enjoying the attractions, you'll also learn some cool secrets about the backstage areas. The tour can include up to 12 visitors, so unless you're traveling with a large group, you will most likely share the tour with people you don't know.

The Private VIP Experience is an even more exclusive (and expensive) tour for just you and your party, in which you get to dictate what rides you want to experience via immediate backdoor access, as well as any special backstage tours, if you want them.

Both VIP Experiences offer meet-and-greets with characters like Doctor Doom, and behind-the-scenes experiences, such as standing underneath the ride track in Revenge of the Mummy while you watch riders experience a "false end," or a special tour of the Immigration Room inside MEN IN BLACK Alien Attack. The packages also include reserved seating for the park's shows and special viewing areas for Universal's Superstar Parade.

One-day, one-park VIP Experience tours are approximately five hours. One-day two-park VIP Experience tours are approximately seven hours. Private VIP Experience tours are approximately eight hours.

After your VIP Experience is over, your VIP card will work as an Express Pass for the rest of the day.

Child Swap

Are you traveling with a young child who can't take part in those thrill rides you're itching to try?

Universal has a child swap option at most attractions. Check with an attendant at the beginning of the queue to be sure. You, your child, and a second adult in your party can proceed through the line to the ride's loading area. Ask for the child swap option when you reach the boarding area. One adult can stay with the child in the child swap room while the other rides. When the ride is over, the adults can switch. Oftentimes if you have other children with you, they are allowed to ride twice in a row: once with the first adult and again with the second after the swap. The child swap rooms are usually outfitted with videos or other materials to keep the young child entertained during the wait.

Universal's Photo Connect™ Star Card

Buying a Photo Connect Star Card can be a valuable option if you want to get in on all or many of the staged photo opportunities throughout the parks. Some packages offer digital copies of all the photos taken for you, as well as some fun special effects that can be added to the pictures. You can log on to your account after your visit and order an array of merchandise—such as mugs, ornaments, and mouse pads—featuring your photos. There's even a smartphone app you can use to access your photo account.

Attraction Assistance Pass

If you or someone in your party has a disability that makes it difficult to wait in lines, Universal can provide you with an Attraction Assistance Pass. This pass is not intended to allow immediate access to attractions but it will minimize wait times.

Attraction Assistance Pass holders may enter through an alternate line—such as the Express Pass line—or, if the regular wait time is longer than 30 minutes, the attendant will mark a time on the pass when you can return and use the alternate queue. You can only have one active "reservation" at a time, but you can gain access to alternate lines at other attractions with a wait time of less than 30 minutes.

Visit Guest Services inside the park to request a pass. It's recommended that you bring a letter from your doctor describing your physical limitations. The Guest Services employee has the authority to determine whether you meet Universal's requirements for the pass.

American Express® Lounge

If you are an American Express cardholder, be sure to bring your card with you. Members receive 10 percent off at many restaurants and can take a break at the American Express Lounge in Universal Studios Florida near the Shrek 4-D attraction. Inside the air-conditioned lounge you'll find complimentary light snacks, drinks, a television, charging stations, and comfortable seating while you take a breather.

Merchandise Pickup

If you'd like to do some shopping inside the parks but don't want to carry your items around for the rest of the day, Universal offers free delivery of purchases to the exit gates, so you can pick up your parcels upon leaving. If you are staying at one of Universal's on-site hotels, you can even arrange for purchased items to be delivered to your hotel.

CHAPTER ONE

UNIVERSAL STUDIOS FLORIDA

UNIVERSAL STUDIOS FLORIDA IS A compact park, with each attraction only a stone's throw from the next. The theming here is based on Universal's movie studio background, with most of the "lands" themed as a movie "backlot" (a large, exterior set used for filming). Some sets are completely imaginary; others are meant to replicate a specific location, such as New York City. As you move through these backlots and lands, you'll often find an abundance of little details to keep you engaged and entertained.

The addition of The Wizarding World of Harry Potter—Diagon Alley, including the Hogwarts Express, in the summer of 2014 has further increased the park's popularity. Other well-loved attractions include Hollywood Rip Ride Rockit, Despicable Me Minion Mayhem, Revenge of the Mummy, TRANSFORMERS: The Ride-3D, MEN IN BLACK Alien Attack, and The Simpsons Ride.

Universal Studios Florida basically encompasses a large circle, so if you start at one end and work your way around, you'll have a hard time missing something on your list. With seven themed lands, 14 rides, seven shows, two play areas, eating, shopping, and even occasional street parades, street shows, and character meet-and-greets, there's plenty to take in.

If you follow the clockwise path, you'll first encounter Production Central, then you'll move on to New York, San Francisco, The Wizarding World of Harry Potter, World Expo, Woody Woodpecker's Kid-Zone, and finally, Hollywood.

If you've got young children, visit Production Central first and then follow a counterclockwise path. This means heading into Hollywood on the right after Production Central, which would lead you to Woody Woodpecker's KidZone—including Animal Actors on Location! and E.T. Adventure—more quickly. If it's thrill rides you're after, take the clockwise route that sends you on a more direct path to the Rip Ride Rockit, TRANSFORMERS: The Ride-3D, and Revenge of the Mummy. The Wizarding World of Harry Potter—Diagon Alley is near the middle of the circle, so there is no real shortcut to get there.

As a parent, I personally prefer to take the clockwise route, leaving the Woody Woodpecker's KidZone for later in the day. I can take a breather while the kids get a chance to run around.

Next we'll break down these varied backlots and lands, along with the attractions within each, following the "thrill seekers" clockwise route. The following tips and secrets will help you navigate your way through Universal Studios Florida and make the most of your time in the park.

IT'S A FACT

WHO DOESN'T LOVE A PARADE?

Universal stages a daily character-packed parade inside the park, which features elaborately designed floats, each themed for a specific set of characters. The parade also includes professional dancers, aerial stunt performers, and even a live drum line led by Hop's E.B. The parade makes regular stops at Mel's Drive-In and Battery Park, so visitors get the chance to interact with favorite characters.

The characters in Universal's Superstar Parade are usually scheduled to step out near Mel's Drive-In (Hollywood) before the parade as well. This provides for a more intimate meet-and-greet where you can take pictures with the characters. Times vary so check with an attendant.

TACTICAL **TIP**

LET THE KIDS BLOW OFF SOME STEAM

If your kids need to let out some steam while at Universal Studios Florida, check out Woody Woodpecker's KidZone. Young kids will love unleashing all that energy in Fievel's Playland, Barney's Backyard, and the Curious George Goes to Town play area.

Although they can't run free and climb there, there's certainly a great deal to explore in The Wizarding World of Harry Potter – Diagon Alley as well.

LOOK FOR THE SIDE ENTRANCE

If the entrance lines are very long when you arrive at the park—and you've already purchased your tickets—head to the second, lesser-known entrance by the Blue Man Group attraction. Follow the path from Universal's CityWalk toward the Blue Man Group theater. You'll see it right by the Rip Ride Rockit roller coaster.

Note: This entrance isn't always accessible when the park first opens.

A TRIBUTE TO MOVIE-MAKING (WITH FIREWORKS!)

The evening spectacular at Universal Studios Florida is a tribute to the company's "100 Years of Movie Memories." Large screens showcase a slew of Universal films, from the old-fashion silent pictures all the way up to present-day films. The presentation is narrated by actor Morgan Freeman. Water effects and lights add excitement to the show, and it is topped off with a fireworks display.

TACTICAL **TIP**

MAKE THE MOST OF ONE DAY: THRILL SEEKERS AND OLDER FAMILIES

If you're heading to Universal Studios Florida for just one day and want to fill it with thrills, chills, and laughs, this list is for you. These are the most popular attractions in the park for older visitors…

- Despicable Me Minion Mayhem
- Hollywood Rip Ride Rockit
- TRANSFORMERS: The Ride-3D
- Revenge of the Mummy
- Disaster! – A Major Motion Picture Ride…Starring You
- All of The Wizarding World of Harry Potter – Diagon Alley

- MEN IN BLACK Alien Attack
- The Simpsons Ride
- Horror Make-Up Show
- Universal's Cinematic Spectacular in the evening before the park closes

More Fun (if you have the time)

- TWISTER...Ride It Out
- Terminator 2: 3-D
- Shrek 4-D
- Animal Actors on Location!
- Beetlejuice Graveyard Revue
- Universal's Superstar Parade (If you aren't a parade fan, use this time to catch one of the more popular attractions as lines may be shorter.)

TACTICAL **TIP**

MAKE THE MOST OF ONE DAY: NON-THRILL SEEKERS AND YOUNG FAMILIES

If you're heading to Universal Studios Florida with your young family for just one day, review this list. These are the most beloved attractions in the park for young families, and these attractions provide a balance of rides and play areas so your kids can let out some energy stored up from waiting in so many lines throughout the day...

- Despicable Me Minion Mayhem
- Shrek 4-D
- TRANSFORMERS: The Ride-3D (if party is old enough)
- TWISTER...Ride It Out (very young children may be afraid)

- All of The Wizarding World of Harry Potter – Diagon Alley (Escape from Gringotts may be too intense for some)
- MEN IN BLACK Alien Attack
- Kang & Kodos' Twirl 'n' Hurl
- All of Woody Woodpecker's KidZone
- Universal's Superstar Parade (If you aren't a parade fan, use this time to catch one of the more popular attractions as lines may be shorter.)
- Universal's Cinematic Spectacular in the evening before the park closes

PRODUCTION CENTRAL

Right past the entrance gates you'll find yourself inside Production Central. This first "backlot" of the park, themed with soundstages to give it a film production feel, houses several of the most popular attractions at Universal Studios Florida: Despicable Me Minion Mayhem, Hollywood Rip Ride Rockit, TRANSFORMERS: The Ride-3D, and the very family-friendly Shrek 4-D.

Despicable Me Minion Mayhem

First up is the Despicable Me Minion Mayhem 3-D ride. If you've got Despicable Me fans in your party, this is a must-see. You'll start your adventure in "Gru's home" (a large waiting room), where Gru appears on a screen to explain that you have been recruited to take part in his latest experiment: to transform people into minions and train them to work for him. Then, you'll head inside the main room, which is equipped with motion ride benches paired with 3-D glasses for a hilarious adventure with Margo, Edith, Agnes, Gru, and the minions.

Note: There are stationary benches in the front of the room for those who'd like to enjoy the attraction without motion. Be sure to tell the attendant you want the stationary seating when entering the line; it may cut your wait time.

Shrek 4-D

Shrek, Donkey, and Fiona appear larger than life in Universal's Shrek 4-D attraction. Fiona has been captured again, and it's up to Shrek and Donkey to rescue her. You'll start off in the late Lord Farquaad's (now a ghost) secret chamber with the three little pigs and the gingerbread man. Then you'll move inside to the main room and join Shrek in a high-speed pursuit of Fiona and her captors. This motion bench ride takes you galloping through forests, riding on a dragon, and plunging down a waterfall. To help make the experience extra exciting, the motion ride is also equipped to spray water and mist, and create wind.

Hollywood Rip Ride Rockit

If you're a thrill seeker, you'll love the Hollywood Rip Ride Rockit roller coaster. Many consider this wildly popular attraction to be Universal Orlando's best coaster. It's an intense ride that takes you on a heart-thumping 90-degree incline up 17 stories high and has what Universal calls the world's first "non-inverting loop." It also provides multisensory excitement, as you'll rock out to the song of your choice; music comes booming from a surround-sound system built right into your coaster seat.

Your experience is also video-recorded. You can purchase a copy to take home and relive your Rip Ride moment. Some riders complain that as this coaster has aged, it has become more jarring to your body. Sitting near the front of the car makes the ride a little smoother. You can ask the attendant if you can wait for a front car seat.

TRANSFORMERS: The Ride-3D

This technologically advanced 3-D motion simulator ride may have you feeling as though you jumped straight into an actual *Transformers* movie yourself. You'll journey through an epic battle between the Transformers and the Decepticons for possession of the all-important "Allspark." During the elaborately detailed queue (which helps you endure the long wait for this attraction), video monitors fill you in on the backstory. The Allspark must be protected at all costs from the evil Decepticons, and you, the completely new recruits, have been ordered to engage in the battle as a last resort. Your vehicle—an Autobot named Evac—is able to intercept the Allspark from a Decepticon's grasp. The adventure ramps up from there with 3-D graphics, twists, spins, turns, and extensive stage design that's so authentic you may just forget it isn't real. The technology behind this ride is similar to The Amazing Adventures of Spider-Man attraction in Islands of Adventure.

Dining and Shopping in Production Central

To grab a bite to eat, head to Production Central's Classic Monsters Café, which serves lunch and dinner. There's also the Bone Chillin' beverage kiosk, serving adults beer, mixed drinks, and slushies. If you have a sweet tooth, check out Studio Suites for candies, homemade fudge, cotton candy, and baked treats.

Shopping opportunities include the Universal Studios store for general park merchandise, the Supply Vault for Transformers merchandise, Super Silly Stuff for Despicable Me products, and Shrek's Ye Olde Souvenir Shoppe.

TACTICAL **TIP**

SHORTEN THE WAIT AT DESPICABLE ME MINION MAYHEM

If you'd like to experience the Despicable Me Minion Mayhem attraction but the wait time is outside your comfort zone, there may be a way around it. Ask the attendant if you can go to the stationary seating line. Stationary seating benches do not move like the standard motion benches in this attraction, but still provide an enjoyable experience in a less intense way. Choosing stationary seating can sometimes shoot you straight to the front of the queue.

SHH... IT'S A SECRET

ORLANDO
FLORIDA

DID YOU KNOW THAT DURING YOUR INTENSE 3-D ADVENTURE INSIDE TRANSFORMERS: THE RIDE-3D, YOUR CAR ACTUALLY MOVES BETWEEN TWO DIFFERENT FLOORS?

Your vehicle enters an elevator to go up a level, and then later on, another lift takes you back down. It's so ingeniously designed, you may not even notice when this happens, especially since the screens in front of you move with the vehicle.

IT'S A FACT

HOLLYWOOD RIP RIDE ROCKIT STATS

I bet you didn't know these cool statistics about the Hollywood Rip Ride Rockit…

- This roller coaster climbs a breathtaking 17 stories in the air.

- It has an intense 90-degree lift hill (that's straight up). (A lift hill is the first large hill on a coaster where the cars are mechanically pulled to the top.)

- This coaster features three unique maneuvers: the Treble Clef (built to replicate the musical symbol), the Double Take (the largest non-inverted loop in the world), and the Jump Cut (a spiraling negative-gravity move).

- The original design of the music-inspired Treble Clef was sketched out on a paper napkin.

- The coaster reaches top speeds of 65mph.

- This ride features six near-miss moments (which is when two cars seem as though they are about to collide, but veer away from each other at the last moment).

- It has the world's first non-inverting loop.

- This coaster cost $45 million to build.

- It can accommodate 1,850 passengers per hour.

IT'S A
FACT

DO YOU RECOGNIZE THE VOICE?

Shrek fans will immediately recognize the voices in Shrek 4-D as those of the original stars of the movies: Mike Myers as Shrek, Eddie Murphy as Donkey, Cameron Diaz as Princess Fiona, and John Lithgow as Lord Farquaad.

If you have a good ear for voices, you may also notice that the Despicable Me Minion Mayhem attraction features the original actors from these beloved movies, including Steve Carell as Gru, Miranda Cosgrove as Margo, Dana Gaier as Edith, and Elsie Fisher as Agnes.

SHH... IT'S A SECRET

ORLANDO FLORIDA

PICK SECRET SONGS FOR YOUR ROLLER COASTER RIDE

Before you ride Hollywood Rip Ride Rockit, think about this list of secret music accompaniments online. The list is extensive, but if you choose your song ahead of time, you'll be ready when the time comes (when songlist is unavailable, a random track will be selected for you). Once on the ride—but before you begin your vertical climb—hold the Rockit logo for 5 to 10 seconds. It will bring up a number pad. Enter in the three-digit number of your chosen hidden track.

The secret song list currently includes "Save Room" by John Legend (309), "The Thrill Is Gone" by BB King (506), "Cyanide" by Metallica (701), "Immigrant Song" by Led Zeppelin (113), and "Start Me Up" by the Rolling Stones (122).

Universal Studios Florida

TACTICAL **TIP**

THE BEST SEATS IN THE EVAC AUTOBOT

You'll have a more panoramic view in the front three rows of the TRANSFORMERS: The Ride-3D, but for a more intense 3-D experience—and a less queasy stomach—shoot for the middle and back rows.

NEW YORK

The New York section of Universal Studios Florida is full of interesting Big Apple-inspired sets, such as the New York Public Library and Park Avenue circa the 1930s and 1940s. Building facades include an old-fashioned Macy's store, the Metropolis Tribune (a nod to Superman), and the Kitty Kat Club, which is a hat tip to the Broadway musical *Cabaret*.

Although you won't find a slew of attractions here, New York offers some memorable photo opps against these iconic backgrounds, and you can catch some street shows. The two main attractions in New York are TWISTER...Ride It Out and the exciting Revenge of the Mummy. As of press time, there's a rumor that TWISTER... Ride It Out may close and be replaced with a new attraction. However, there are no official details available at this time.

TWISTER...Ride It Out

This show is designed around the movie *Twister*, starring Helen Hunt and Bill Paxton. After some initial queue rooms with props and screens presenting clips from the movie, the last prop room shows a video narrated by Hunt and Paxton that discusses the movie and facts about tornadoes. You'll then be ushered into the main show room, where you'll stand in one of three rows. From here, you'll view a two- to three-minute simulation of what it's like to witness a category F5 twister's vortex up close. Props on stage will fly around; you'll see some fire, and even an explosion. You may get misted in the process— especially if you're in the back row.

Revenge of the Mummy

Beware of the dangers lurking inside the Revenge of the Mummy's indoor, mostly dark, roller coaster ride. For folks unsure if they can handle it, this fairly intense experience is similar to the park's Hollywood Rip Ride Rockit. You'll start the Revenge experience in some thoughtfully staged rooms to set the mood and story, in which you've been lucky enough to be selected as an extra for the new *Revenge of the Mummy* movie. As you can guess, this isn't the real deal, and very soon, things take a very dark turn when you begin to speed along the coaster's track, attempting to escape the evil clutches of the mummy, Imhotep.

The Blues Brothers Show

If you're a Blues Brothers fan, slide down to Delancey Street for the daily Blues Brothers Show. Opening for the famous duo is a sassy blues singer, Mabel the waitress, accompanied by her sax-playing pal, Jazz. Then the Blues Brothers (though obviously they are not the original actors) sing and dance. During the holiday season the songs are modified to include numbers like "Snow Man." This show doesn't run every day, so be sure to check the park's schedule if you have your heart set on seeing it.

Dining and Shopping in New York

There are two restaurants in New York where you can enjoy lunch or dinner. One is Louie's Italian Restaurant for standard Italian fare; the other is Finnegan's Bar and Grill, where you'll find an Irish-American menu. You can also grab a coffee at Starbuck's, or some ice cream at Ben & Jerry's.

For shopping, try Aftermath at the exit of TWISTER...Ride It Out. The store features Twister-related merchandise along with other Universal favorites, and Sahara Traders offers Revenge of the Mummy souvenirs to take home.

INSIDE REVENGE OF THE MUMMY

Here are some insider details you might not guess about this attraction...

- Designers made sure the ancient hieroglyphics on the walls actually spell out words and warnings.

- You can see a tribute to the previous attraction—Kongfrontation—at this location. In the queue, look to the left in the "gold room" and you'll see a golden statue of King Kong sitting on a cabinet.

- Because the track for Kongfrontation was part of the building itself, there are still pieces of it inside this attraction.

- Brace yourself for some unexpected pyrotechnics during the ride.

TAKE THE CONTROL ROOM TOUR

If you ask the TWISTER…Ride It Out attendant, he or she may take you behind the scenes to visit the control room where special effects are generated during the show. The technicians will let you in on some of the details and then you can step into a viewing area to watch them reset the stage for the next run-through. Then, stay to watch the show yourself.

IT'S A
FACT

HOW TWISTER...RIDE IT OUT WAS CREATED

This indoor simulation shows you what it feels like to witness a category F5 tornado. Here are some fun facts about the creation of this experience...

- Each minute of full-force air used during the show is equal to the amount of air it would take to fill more than four full-size blimps.

- At 110 decibels, TWISTER's sound effects are blasted through a 42,000-watt sound system consisting of more than 50 speakers. That's so loud it's equal to the sound levels at a rock concert.

- The attraction's simulated tornado is the largest indoor twister ever created. This impressive man-made funnel cloud is approximately five stories tall and 12 feet wide.

- The address on the firehouse facade of TWISTER…Ride It Out was originally 9-1-1, but was changed to 2-9-1 following the September 11th attacks on the United States in 2001.

SAN FRANCISCO

The San Francisco backlot is packed with "local" attractions, such as cable car tracks and a turnaround, a replica of the famous Fisherman's Wharf sign, and a small but scenic waterfont. Many of this section's visuals bow to the 1974 movie *Earthquake*, and this area really capitalizes on the earthquake theme throughout. Even inside Richter Burger Co., the menu hawks burgers with names like "the Fault Line" and "Aftershock."

Inside this themed land you can also visit Beetlejuice Graveyard Revue, and Disaster! – A Major Motion Picture Ride...Starring YOU attractions. This section was previously called "San Francisco/Amity" but was renamed when the Jaws attraction closed. You can still catch a tribute to the great white's terror at the dock, where a giant shark hangs upside down.

Beetlejuice Graveyard Revue

Many folks who've been to Universal Orlando Resort several times have never checked out Beetlejuice Graveyard Revue. Some consider this show simply as a means to escape the heat, an opportunity to rest, or a place to kill time before enjoying another attraction. But, insiders will tell you that this show is underrated. It started as a street show and was so well-received, Universal decided to move it indoors with its own set and an improved sound system. Starring the crazy but electrifying title character from the *Beetlejuice* movie, the show incorporates classic Hollywood monsters such as the Werewolf, Frankenstein, Dracula, and the Bride of Frankenstein. There's no real storyline here, but you will catch lots of Beetlejuice-style laughs (some jokes are raunchy), singing, and awesome dance moves. This is a loud, rockin', crazy show for the young at heart but perhaps not too young of age.

Disaster! – A Major Motion Picture Ride...Starring YOU

This is one of Universal's true "ride the movies" attractions, where you can also learn some of the tricks used to make films. Part show, part ride, this attraction packs laughs and excitement into one experience. First you'll see live demonstrations of exciting stunts and special effects used in movies, employing people right from the audience. Then you'll board subway cars to act as extras in a simulated earthquake subway scene. Be sure to catch the movie trailer at the end starring Duane "The Rock" Johnson...and you.

Dining and Shopping in San Francisco

San Francisco offers Universal Studio Florida's premiere restaurant for full-service dining, Lombard's Seafood Grille. You can enjoy Lombard's yummy menu with views of the lagoon. For a quicker, less-expensive option, head to the earthquake-themed Richter's Burger Co. There's also Chez Alcatraz, an outdoor drink stand (open seasonally), where you can buy mixed drinks, frozen drinks, and snacks.

Shopping options are limited in San Francisco. The San Francisco Candy Factory is a good source for sweets, such as fudge and candy apples, but you'll need to head to another land for Universal-themed gifts.

TACTICAL **TIP**

GET PICKED TO BE AN EXTRA!

One of the secrets to getting picked as a movie extra at the Disaster! attraction is to stand up front and act as animated as possible so the ride lead will notice you. (The ride lead oversees the operations of the ride/show and is the one who picks folks from the audience.)

Note: Every ride lead picks differently so there's no guarantee you will be chosen.

WHO'S THE UPSIDE DOWN MAN?

If you pop inside Richter's Burger Co. you can't miss the 10-foot-tall upside down statue of a man who's apparently missing his head. (The implication is, his head is stuck in the floor.) There's no sign to explain it. So, what in the world is this about? The upside down man is a replica of the famous Professor Agassiz statue (at Stanford University), which fell during the 1906 San Francisco earthquake. The statue's head smashed through the ground below and the "man" stood upside down just as the statue inside Richter's does today.

WORLD EXPO

When Universal Orlando Florida opened its doors, the World Expo section was designed to showcase both futuristic and retro themes. It originally took on a 1964 World's Fair atmosphere. This fit well with the original time travel-themed Back to the Future: The Ride attraction, and later on with the installation of the current MEN IN BLACK Alien Attack attraction. In fact, you'll even see a model of the 1964 World's Fair observation towers, which were featured in one of the *Men in Black* movies. This area still works well for the Men in Black attraction, but also now includes the Springfield USA area dedicated to "The Simpsons" television show. (Springfield USA replaced Back to the Future: The Ride.) Marrying the Men in Black to the Springfield USA is a bit of a stretch. These two areas feel more like separate sections and don't easily create one single identity for World Expo.

Fear Factor Live

Fear Factor Live is just as the title suggests: a live version of the game show. If you're a fan of the gross and scary stunts regularly shown on the television version, you'll want to catch the live show. Six contestants are preselected to compete in Fear Factor Live, and several volunteers from the audience are selected to "help" (or rather hinder) the contestants as they try to reach their goals. Contestants do the "walk of shame" if they fail at stunts, which are performed at dangerous heights and involve interacting with creepy crawly creatures. If you want to be a contestant, arrive about 70 minutes before the show and tell the attendant you'd like to compete. You'll need a photo ID, and it usually helps if you happen to be in good physical shape. This show is categorized as seasonal, so it may not be open during your visit.

MEN IN BLACK Alien Attack

This very popular ride starts out with a large room featuring "The Universe and You" 1964 World's Fair science exhibit. Soon it becomes apparent that this is a front for recruiting the Men in Black corps. As you enter the long line, you'll get a chance to enjoy some interesting details from the films. You eventually board vehicles for a training session (shooting aliens), but quickly hear an announcement that the rookies are needed for an all-out alien emergency. Your vehicle whisks you into another area for a full-on defense mission. Then you'll experience a super fun, frenzied time shooting every alien you can locate to rack up points and save the world. Each rider is given an individual score, and your vehicle competes with the vehicle launched simultaneously with yours. This giant immersive, addictive video game is a blast for all ages.

Because this is a favorite ride for groups, the single rider line usually allows for a much shorter wait time if you don't mind riding alone. If you choose the single rider line, you aren't allowed to request to ride with a specific person, but sometimes you end up in the same vehicle anyway.

Kang & Kodos' Twirl 'n' Hurl

Don't be scared off by the name. This gentle spinning lift ride—styled in the shape of aliens Kang & Kodos from The Simpsons—is a great alternative for young Simpsons fans who aren't ready for the slightly more stomach-churning Simpsons Ride. The ride is similar to Islands of Adventure's One Fish, Two Fish, Red Fish, Blue Fish attraction within Seuss Landing. You pilot flying saucers with humorous names such as HindenBorg, Old Ironglorp, and Citizen Kang.

The Simpsons Ride

Are you ready for an intense, funny simulator thrill ride, Simpsons-style? This beloved attraction offers a major payoff—even if you aren't a big Simpsons fan. Inside the queue, you'll learn Krusty the Clown is going to open his own amusement park (yikes!) and an old "friend" is out to spoil the fun. The Simpson family (and you as well) are the lucky first-time riders on Krusty's roller coaster. You'll move into one of several simulation rooms and slide into your "car." From here, this crazy, sometimes stomach-churning simulation ride may have you convinced you're really along on the Simpsons' insane adventure. The ride itself is exciting, though a little jarring, as simulator rides go. Keep in mind that although this isn't a real coaster, it can cause motion-sickness.

Dining and Shopping in World Expo

Inside World Expo, you can eat like the Simpsons at Fast Food Boulevard. This is a food court setup with options like Lisa's Teahouse of Horror, Luigi's, The Frying Dutchman, Cletus' Chicken Shack, and Krustyburger. You can sit in the main seating area or take your food into Moe's Tavern. Outdoors, there's also Duff Brewery's beer garden for drinks and snacks, Lard Lad Donuts for donuts and ice cream, and Bumblebee Man's Taco Truck for, obviously, tacos.

For shopping, Men in Black fans can head to the MIB Gear Shop, and Simpsons afficionados can check out the Kwik-E-Mart for a wonderful overdose of Springfield USA merchandise.

SIMPSONS SECRETS

Here are some interesting facts about
The Simpsons Ride...

- The clips in the video you'll watch
  while in line, featuring some of your
  favorite Simpsons characters, were
  designed specifically for the attraction.

- All voices in this ride feature the
  original actors, including Dan
  Castellaneta as Homer Simpson and
  Krusty the Clown, Nancy Cartwright
  as Bart Simpson and Maggie
  Simpson, Julie Kavner as Marge
  Simpson, and Yeardley Smith as
  Lisa Simpson.

- Even though your vehicle never moves more than two feet in any direction, you may feel as though you've ridden a real roller coaster.

- The immense wraparound screen has great high-definition graphics for high impact, which helps convince your mind—and stomach—that you're going along on the crazy ride the Simpsons are experiencing.

IT'S A FACT

BACK TO THE SIMPSONS

The original ride system from Back to the Future: The Ride is still in use. The replacement attraction, The Simpsons Ride, utilizes the original architecture for its newer Simpsons-themed experience. Although you feel like you are in an individual simulator because you pile into separate rooms, this attraction really hosts 12 cars in front of one gigantic screen.

SPRINGFIELD USA PAYPHONE

If you pay a visit to the famous Kwik-E-Mart in the Simpsons-inspired Springfield USA section of World Expo, take a moment to stand by the pay phone out front. You'll notice a picture of bully Nelson Muntz "suggesting" you answer the phone. When it rings, be sure to pick it up and listen for a message from a famous Springfield resident.

TACTICAL **TIP**

THE BEST SEAT FOR
THE SIMPSONS RIDE

The best seat for this attraction is also the one that produces less motion sickness (for those prone to it). You'll want to shoot for Room Six, on Level Two, which is the middle vehicle on the middle level of the attraction's dome. When you approach the first split in the line, kindly ask the attendant for Level Two, then request Room Six of the next attendant. (You may need to wait a little longer because of your request.)

TOUR THE IMMIGRATION ROOM

The replica of the Immigration Room in the *Men in Black* movies that you look down on as you wait in line for the attraction can actually be toured. Ask an attendant if Immigration Room tours are being conducted that day. A special guide will take you into this room, where you can get a close-up view of what went into creating this part of the attraction. You'll see Men in Black paperwork and magazines featuring alien sightings on the desks. You'll have a better chance of scoring this special tour during slow times at the attraction.

SCORE BIG INSIDE MEN IN BLACK ALIEN ATTACK

Hoping to rack up some big points inside MEN IN BLACK Alien Attack? Here are some tips…

- You'll score a lot of points if you can find and shoot Frank the Pug with your laser gun. He's hidden in the second room, on the right-hand side in the newspaper stand.

- Try to hit your opponent's green light at the bottom of their vehicle.

- Listen for Agent K's prompt to press that red button (yes, the very one he tells you repeatedly not to push). Hit it at just the right moment to grab an extra 100,000 points.

Universal Studios Florida

- Hold the trigger button on your weapon down the entire time.
- Aim between the aliens' red eyes.
- Shoot aliens multple times when possible.
- If you shoot your opponent's car (aim for the red light at the top); it will cause it to spin and gain points for you at the same time.

WOODY WOODPECKER'S KIDZONE

While many folks think that Universal Orlando's amusement parks are geared solely toward adults and older kids, there are many attractions to satisfy young visitors. Woody Woodpecker's KidZone is an enjoyable area designed for younger children with plenty of space for little ones to run around, enjoy some rides that are just their speed, and allow tired parents to rest in the shade. Inside this area, you can visit the popular Animal Actors on Location! show, A Day in the Park with Barney, Curious George Goes to Town, Woody Woodpecker's Nuthouse Coaster, Fievel's Playland, and the E.T. Adventure attraction.

> *Note: At the time this book was printed, there were rumors Universal was planning to renovate or replace the Woody Woodpecker's KidZone, but no details were officially confirmed by the resort.*

Animal Actors on Location!

Animal Actors on Location! is a crowd-pleaser for all ages and features trained animals that fly, crawl, slither, walk, and everything in between. Well scripted and designed—like so many of Universal Orlando Resort's shows—Animal Actors on Location! incorporates creatures, volunteers, loads of jokes, unexpected surprises, video clips, and behind-the-scenes secrets about how animals are trained to behave in certain ways. The 20-minute show is just short enough for young kids to sit through and long enough for families to get a break from the sun.

E.T. Adventure

This sweet, gentle ride starring E.T. from Steven Spielberg's blockbuster movie is a hit with fans, especially young ones. Board your "bicycle," which is actually a 12-passenger gondola with E.T.-style seating, for a trip to bring E.T. home to his planet. You'll fly over woods, then "up in the stars," and eventually to the Green Planet to deliver E.T. and save the day. Note that this attraction may not be that easy to relate to if you haven't seen the movie first. Also, young children may be a little afraid in the first few dark areas, but overall it's a cute story and appealing to young visitors.

Fievel's Playland

This interactive play area is a great stop for families with younger kids who will love the chance to run, explore, jump, slide, and just be a kid. Although amusement park rides are fun, parents know all too well that a day at a theme park can mean a lot of waiting and sitting for little ones. This area offers kids a chance to let all that energy

out while worn-out parents catch their breath. Fievel's Playland is modeled after the animated character Fievel the mouse, from the films *An American Tail* and *Fievel Goes West*. You can explore the area from a mouse's point of view, which means all the objects inside—such as a cowboy hat and boots—are super-sized. There's even a 200-foot-long waterslide.

Woody Woodpecker's Nuthouse Coaster

Here's a great beginner's roller coaster to prime your young kids for Universal's intense coasters when they grow older. This ride lasts for only about a minute, and offers enough thrills and chills for little ones to get in on the excitement of Universal Studios Florida. This coaster is designed to look as though Woody Woodpecker used his zany creativity to build it from spare parts at a nut-processing factory.

A Day in the Park with Barney

This show is centered around the superstar that all toddlers love: Barney and his friends. If you've got Barney fans, they'll love this show filled with singing and dancing, showcasing many of Barney's well-known songs. After the show is over, kids get a chance to meet Barney and get a picture. There's also a wonderful play area in the back called Barney's Backyard, where kids will be ushered after the performance. This indoor play area is filled with kid-friendly activities, such as sand play, water play, making music, climbing, exploring, and more. Young kids will love a chance to move around and explore while parents get an opportunity to rest.

Curious George Goes to Town

This is the largest play area inside Woody Woodpecker's KidZone, full of places to explore, climb, and get wet. Kids, even slightly older ones, love the water cannons, streams of water shooting in all directions, and giant water buckets that dump occasionally onto excited visitors. In the back, there's also a fun-filled, two-story Ball Factory where you can shoot foam balls all around with Auto Blasters. For any active, hot kid, this is the perfect place to unleash some energy and cool down at the same time. There's no time limit and some kids may want to spend nearly all day here so be sure to time your visit around what works best for your group. Many folks like to hit this area before lunch or right before leaving the park at the end of the day.

Dining and Shopping in Woody Woodpecker's KidZone

When it's time to eat, you can head to the Kid Zone Pizza Company for quick service options such as pizza, chicken fingers, and fruit cups.

Shopping options include SpongeBob StorePants for SpongeBob merchandise, the Barney Store for little fans of the big purple dinosaur, and E.T.'s Toy Closet & Photo Spot for all your E.T. items as well as a memorable E.T.'s closet photo op.

TACTICAL **TIPS**

THE SIDE DOOR TO BARNEY'S BACKYARD

Does your child want to return to Barney's Backyard for more playtime? You can enter Barney's Backyard through a side entrance any time your child wants to explore the area. This is also a nice spot to stop when you need to get out of the sun and into an air-conditioned space.

BEST SEATS INSIDE E.T. ADVENTURE

If you're looking for the best seat on the E.T. Adventure attraction, the left-hand side of the gondola offers the best views of the starlit city and other areas of the ride, especially from the front row.

IT'S A
FACT

THE FIRST UNIVERSAL ATTRACTION TO GET AN ORIGINAL SCORE

Can you guess which attraction at Universal Orlando Florida was the first to get its own original musical score? Composer John Williams, who wrote the music for films such as *E.T.*, *Jaws*, *Star Wars Episode V: The Empire Strikes Back*, *Raiders of the Lost Ark*, and more, lent his talents to write the music for the E.T. Adventure. This was the first time an original music score was included in an attraction's design.

TACTICAL **TIP**

TAKE A MEMORABLE PHOTO
INSIDE E.T.'S TOY CLOSET

If you have an E.T. fan, you won't want to
miss the photo opportunites in the post-ride
shop connected to E.T. Adventure. Look for
E.T.'s Toy Closet, just like the closet from the
original movie, and the fan-favorite bike-flying
scene where you can pose with your favorite
extraterrestrial.

CURIOUS GEORGE GOES
TO TOWN

Here are a couple tips for parents to help the whole family make the most of this inviting play area …

- Kids can get pretty soaked in a short period of time hanging out at Curious George Goes to Town. Bring a towel and even a change of clothes if the weather is on the cool side.

- There are special "dry-zone" footprints along the ground leading to the Ball Factory for those who want to stay dry, although getting splashed is often part of the fun for kids.

- Many people like to time a visit here just before lunch or at the end of the day.

- It may be smart to hit some of your "bucket list" attractions before you visit Curious George Goes to Town. Many kids beg to stay in this area for as long as you'll let them.

TACTICAL **TIP**

A 1,000-GALLON COWBOY HAT AND A 30-FOOT SPIDER WEB

Where will you find these larger-than-life items, just waiting to be climbed? Check out Fievel's Playland, where everything is from Fievel the mouse's perspective, and therefore ordinary things are now super-sized, such as a book titled *Life and Times of Wylie Burp*, a ladle, pair of glasses, a cowboy boot, and a newspaper.

HOLLYWOOD

Hollywood is one of the smaller backlots at Universal, stretching just two blocks. This land pays homage to the golden age of Hollywood, with building facades that look like the famous 1940s nightclubs Mocambo and Ciro's. You'll see a mini walk of fame along the sidewalk, and even a gorgeous, though much smaller, incredibly detailed replica of the Beverly Wilshire Hotel. Toward the end of the Hollywood backlot, you'll notice the intriguing Garden of Allah Villas building, which at first looks like a restaurant. Actually, it's just an interesting facade referencing Hollywood's original Garden of Allah Villas, which housed writers and actors from the 1930s through the 1950s. Theming aside, you can catch Terminator 2: 3-D – Battle Across Time attraction, the entertaining Universal Orlando's Horror Make-Up Show, and Lucy – A Tribute, all in this area of the park.

Terminator 2: 3-D – Battle Across Time

This attraction is a memorable experience, especially for Terminator fans, although the pre-show presentation explains enough for anyone to follow the story. The pre-show sets up the audience for the struggle between corporate bad-guys Cyberdyne and the movie's heroes Sarah Connor and her son, John. You then move into the auditorium to what seem like stationary seats (surprise— they aren't) and you put on your "protective glasses" (think 3-D).

The show is a mix of 3-D imagery and live performance, which makes things very exciting, although the projection quality feels a little dated compared to Universal's other big, visually based attractions. Real stationary seating is available for those who'd rather not feel the motion in this show.

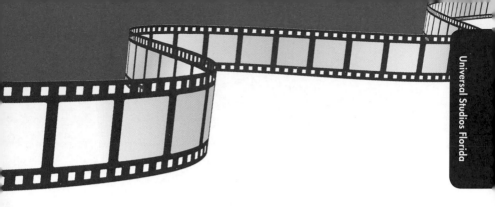

The Universal Horror Make-Up Show

Who better than Universal to combine the artful but gross special effects of horror movies with laugh-out-loud humor? This show is considered by many to be one of Universal's best-kept secrets. The cast is talented at improvising with the "volunteers" from the audience, and there are many surprises in the show. Also, you'll learn a few details about how some of the classic horror effects were created; demonstrations include "slicing" into an arm with a completely dull knife—producing lots of fake blood and a completely intact volunteer. The park suggests parental guidance regarding this show, as some of the humor is a bit adult-oriented, and though the horror effects aren't too offensive, some younger kids may be alarmed.

Lucy – A Tribute

This walk-through museum-style tribute to Lucille Désirée Ball contains a plethora of the star's memorabilia, accompanied by a continuously playing video. The video includes beloved clips of Lucy, and stars Bob Hope and Gale Gordon talking about their memories of her. Young visitors who aren't familiar with Lucille Ball may not be interested in this attraction, but fans of this hilarious lady may find out some interesting facts about her life and get to view some of their favorite scenes.

Dining and Shopping in Hollywood

For dining options in Hollywood, take your pick from Mel's Drive In, Beverly Hills Boulangerie, Schwab's Pharmacy, and Cafe La Bamba.

Mel's Drive-In serves burgers, chicken sandwiches, milk shakes, and more while you rock to the golden oldies. The Beverly Hills Boulangerie is the place to find croissants, sandwiches, soups, and pastries. Schwab's Pharmacy offers milk shakes, banana splits, sundaes, and ice cream floats. Cafe La Bamba offers up ribs, tacos, salads, burritos, and more.

Shopping in Hollywood centers around the Cyber Image, where you can find Terminator memorabilia; the Brown Derby Hat Shop for novelty and character hats, wigs, and visors; and Silver Screen Collectibles, which carries "I Love Lucy" and Betty Boop-themed items and more.

IT'S A
FACT

THE GIANT BROWN HAT

The giant brown hat adorning the Brown Derby Hat Shop is actually much more than just a crafty design. This store pays tribute to Hollywood's famous Brown Derby Restaurant, which was frequented by movie stars such as Clark Gable, Carole Lombard, Cary Grant, Ava Gardner, and Charlie Chaplin. The giant brown hat is a replica of the original Brown Derby building.

CHAPTER TWO

UNIVERSAL'S ISLANDS OF ADVENTURE

ISLANDS OF ADVENTURE MAY BE just a short walk from its sister park Universal Studios Florida, but it certainly has its own identity. When this second park was developed, along with the installation of on-site hotels, Universal solidified itself as a stand-alone vacation destination. Whereas Universal Studios Florida was based on the company's signature movie studio theme, Islands of Adventure takes a very different path with the licensing of an array of characters to create unique themes for each "island."

You'll move from one extremely different island to another; each possesses its own look and feel, featuring high-tech, cutting-edge attractions. The addition of The Wizarding World of Harry Potter – Hogsmeade has further increased the parks popularity and set the bar higher for the next generation of theme-park design.

Inside Islands of Adventure, you'll experience the worlds of Port of Entry, Marvel Super Hero Island, Toon Lagoon, Jurassic Park, The Wizarding World of Harry Potter – Hogsmeade, The Lost Continent, and Seuss Landing. Each island's theming is starkly different from the next, but the transitions are smooth by way of bridges that connect them. Universal Creative, which is Universal's design team, really stepped up the theming in this park; in each island, everywhere you look, the theming carries through to the smallest details, even in the restaurants and shops.

Islands of Adventure has been designed to reach a wide range of park enthusiasts. Universal Orlando Resort is sometimes touted as an amusement resort for adults, but take note there are several areas specifically designed for younger children. Islands of Adventure possesses the Me Ship, The Olive attraction, Camp Jurassic, and the remarkably well-designed, extensive Seuss Landing. Slightly older kids will enjoy many rides and areas of the park as well, including, of course, The Wizarding World of Harry Potter – Hogsmeade.

This area, like its sister park, is laid out in a circle, so if you just move along from island to island, it's hard to miss something. It's also compact like Universal Studios Florida, enabling visitors to see nearly everything on their list in one day. Of course, crowds vary, as do individual must-see lists, so the amount of time needed can vary greatly. This book will take you clockwise through the park, starting with Port of Entry, then Marvel Super Hero Island, Toon Lagoon, Jurassic Park, The Wizarding World of Harry Potter – Hogsmeade, The Lost Continent, and finally Seuss Landing.

Let's start with a few general bits of advice about Islands of Adventure itself.

TACTICAL **TIP**

MAKE THE MOST OF ONE DAY

Thrill-Seekers and Older Families:
If you're traveling with adults only, or older children, here's a list of attractions that will add up to a full day of fun at Islands of Adventure...

- The Incredible Hulk Coaster
- The Amazing Adventures of Spider-Man
- Popeye & Bluto's Bilge-Rat Barges (water ride)
- Dudley Do-Right's Ripsaw Falls (water ride)
- Jurassic Park River Adventure (water ride)
- Dining at Mythos Restaurant
- Poseidon's Fury

- All of The Wizarding World of Harry Potter – Hogsmeade
- Cat in the Hat at Seuss Landing (cute for any Dr. Seuss fan)

More Attractions (if you have time)

- Doctor Doom's Fearfall
- Jurassic Park Discovery Center

Non-Thrill-Seekers:

If you're visiting the park with young children, you can't go wrong with a day filled with the following attractions…

- All of Seuss Landing
- The Eighth Voyage of Sindbad Stunt Show

(continued)

- The Mystic Fountain
- Poseidon's Fury (for slightly older kids)
- Dining at Mythos Restaurant
- All of The Wizarding World of Harry Potter – Hogsmeade, except Dragon Challenge and Forbidden Journey
- Pteranodon Flyers
- Camp Jurassic
- Jurassic Park Discovery Center
- Me Ship, The Olive
- The Amazing Adventures of Spider-Man (40-inch height requirement)

WHERE TO BEAT THE HEAT

These areas of Islands of Adventure can help you beat the heat...

- Seuss Landing's If I Ran the Zoo is a great imaginative play area for young kids to run, explore, slide down tunnels, and get wet.

- Jurassic Park has Camp Jurassic, a shady prehistoric playground where kids can climb nets, cross suspension bridges, and even join a water cannon fight.

- Toon Lagoon has the creative play area Me Ship, The Olive, where youngsters can toot horns, crawl through passageways, get wet, and explore.

(continued)

- Toon Lagoon also has two attractions where kids can get pretty soaked: Dudley Do-Right's Ripsaw Falls and Popeye & Bluto's Bilge-Rat Barges.

- Marvel Super Hero Island has a cool-down misting station right across from The Incredible Hulk Coaster.

BLOW OFF SOME STEAM

There are several places in Islands of Adventure for young children to let out some energy...

- Seuss Landing is full of places for kids to explore, run, and jump, especially If I Ran the Zoo.

- Jurassic Park has Camp Jurassic, which has a large area to explore and climb.

- Toon Lagoon's Me Ship, The Olive is an interactive play area that's full of things to discover.

- The Wizarding World of Harry Potter – Hogsmeade does not possess an interactive play area, but there's room for everyone to stretch their legs.

PORT OF ENTRY

Although Port of Entry lacks attractions all its own, it is Islands of Adventure's first official island, and Universal Creative put a great deal of thought into this entryway to the park. Specifically themed to be your introduction to Islands of Adventure, it is designed to inspire a thirst for adventure with little details everywhere you look. The centerpiece of Port of Entry is Pharos Lighthouse, beckoning explorers far and wide to come experience a day of thrills and excitement.

As you pass through the park entrance turnstiles, you'll stroll under an archway inscribed "The Adventure Begins." Lampposts are adorned with "welcome" messages in multiple languages, there are little jokes to watch for such as the firehouse sign "moving closer to the water," and there are an abundance of references to the other islands in this theme park here.

Also of note in Port of Entry is its music, which was created specially for this island. Many people might not truly notice this unique soundtrack, but it certainly adds to the atmosphere. Take a moment to appreciate all the little things that go into what many consider Orlando's most intricately designed theme park "Main Street."

Dining and Shopping in Port of Entry

There are several dining options in Port of Entry, including Confisco Grille, Croissant Moon Bakery, Cinnabon, and Artic Express.

The Confisco Grille is decorated to reflect all the different islands inside the theme park; this restaurant serves sandwiches, burgers, soups, salads, pasta, and more. Croissant Moon Bakery offers up choices such as deli sandwiches, cheesecakes, and fresh-baked pastries. An American favorite, Cinnabon will satisfy your craving for their pastries. Artic Express provides treats, including root beer floats, waffle cone ice cream, sundaes, and even funnel cakes.

As you can guess, there are also several shopping options in Port of Entry so you can be sure to grab more merchandise on your way out of the park. Islands of Adventure Trading Company provides a wide selection of merchandise from all around the park, including Islands of Adventure logo items. Ocean Trader Market displays an assortment of "imported" items, such as Indian dresses, hats, and jewelry; Indonesian wood carvings; and more. DeFoto's Expedition Photography is the place to go for your camera needs and to pick up your park photo purchases. Port of Entry Christmas Shoppe is a great place to grab an ornament to remember your trip. Island Market and Export Candy Shoppe tempts you with a variety of sweets, including chocolate, cookies, and caramel apples. Lastly, Port Provisions gives you one last chance to purchase a Universal-themed souvenir or gift before heading home.

MARVEL SUPER HERO ISLAND

The island makes fans feel as though they've stepped inside a Marvel comic book. The difficult task here for Universal designers was to tie together what these heroes' worlds have in common, and that was done with great care. Throughout Marvel Super Hero Island there are bold color schemes and architecture, similar to the look of the comic books. You'll also witness giant tributes to your favorite Marvel heroes throughout the island.

In terms of attractions, this is where you'll find some of Universal's most popular thrill rides: The Amazing Adventures of Spider-Man and The Incredible Hulk Coaster along with Doctor Doom's Fearfall and Storm Force Accela-tron. There are also some photo opportunities here with Marvel's beloved characters, several times a day.

The Incredible Hulk Coaster

As you enter the line for this extremely popular attraction, you'll find yourself in Dr. Bruce Banner's lab, where you'll be told you can help him reverse his ability to transform into the Hulk by climbing into the "chamber." (This is, of course, the roller-coaster car.) Things then go terribly wrong, as they so often do, and you are transformed into the Hulk. The Incredible Hulk Coaster is two minutes and 15 seconds of pure thrill, including a zero-to-40mph launch within two seconds, a top speed of 67mph, and seven inversions, including the highest inversion ever built at 109 feet. This is definitely a thrill-seeker's ride.

The Amazing Adventures of Spider-Man

Until the introduction of Harry Potter at Universal Orlando Resort, The Amazing Adventures of Spider-Man was touted as the most technologically advanced, best attraction in the entire theme park world. Some feel it still is. In 2012 it received a significant technological upgrade, making it even more incredible (my apologies to the Hulk). This is considered a 3-D motion simulator ride, taking you along on an unforgettable adventure with Spidey as he saves the city from Dr. Octopus and the Sinister Syndicate.

Doc Oc and his evil crew are using an antigravity gun to steal some of New York's most beloved landmarks in order to get control of the city. Newspaper editor Jameson will draft you as reporters that will help catch the villains and get the scoop for the *Daily Bugle*.

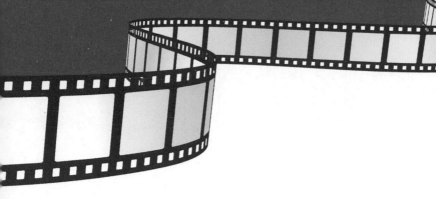

Of course, you'll run into Spider-Man and follow along in this crazy story, nearly getting trapped in Doc Oc's clutches several times.

Spoiler alert: The end of the journey contains a heart-stopping 400-foot sensory drop (not a real one) that leaves you wondering how in the world Universal made it feel so real. This is a must-see for anyone who enjoys a thrill, but it isn't for the very young. You'll need to use your best judgement for younger family members.

Doctor Doom's Fearfall

Doctor Doom is up to his old tricks, and this time he'll use you to take down the Fantastic Four. He intends to extract your fear to create the evil weapon, Fear Juice. This classic freefall ride is just what the Doctor ordered, only with a twist. Unsuspecting riders who love these freefall attractions may be expecting a slow rise and a fast drop, but Doctor Doom knows the element of surprise will get your heart pounding. You'll strap into four-person chair sets and then experience a super high-speed 185-foot launch straight upward, followed by a moment of frightening weightlessness before it drops back down. The ensuing drops are in gentler stages to the platform. The biggest thrill is in the initial launch upwards, so don't hold your breath for a second death-defying drop, as is often the norm with these types of rides.

Storm Force Accelatron

This is a great, classic family ride inside the Marvel world. You'll board this spinning cup ride, aka Professor Xavier's new device, the Accelatron, to help your hero Storm amplify her powers in order to beat super villain Magneto™. Your cup's individual spinning speed can be controlled by you, although you'll be spinning no matter what since your cup is secured to a spinning circular platform that is inside yet a larger spinning circular platform. This is obviously not a great choice for those who tend to get nauseous from twirling.

Dining and Shopping in Marvel Super Hero Island

There are two dining options inside Marvel Super Hero Island, both of which are cafeteria style. Cafe 4 is found inside the Baxter Building, which is the Fantastic Four headquarters and laboratory. There you'll find standard Italian fare, including pizza, meatball subs, spaghetti and meatballs, and chicken Caesar salads. Your second option is the Captain America Diner, serving, as you might guess, an all American-style menu, including cheeseburgers, chicken fingers, chicken sandwiches, and salads.

For shopping, visit four different stores inside Marvel Super Hero Island. To find everything Spider-Man, head straight for the Spider-Man shop. The Marvel Alterniverse Store is full of Marvel superhero collectibles, plus a super-cool photo opp with Spider-Man. The Comic Book Shop is a real comic book store.

SHH... IT'S A SECRET

ORLANDO · FLORIDA

HIDDEN ADAMS

Marvel's own Adam Kubert is the artist who created the marvelous drawings of heroes and super villains you see in Marvel Super Hero Island. Look for the "hidden Adams" (his hidden signature) in each picture. Some are very easy to see, while others can be much trickier. For instance, if you look closely, you'll see "Adam" designed into the Incredible Hulk's thumb and index finger.

UNMARKED PHONES IN MARVEL SUPER HERO ISLAND

There are number of unmarked public phones in Marvel Super Hero Island. These phones are actually interactive. Check them out nearby The Amazing Adventures of Spider-Man, The Incredible Hulk Coaster, and Doctor Doom's Fearfall. Pick up the receiver and hit any button to hear a cool, Marvel-inspired message. Some messages are superhero-oriented and others are centered around villains. It's worth a quick stop—especially for young fans.

TACTICAL **TIP**

BEST PHOTO OPP AT MARVEL SUPER HERO ISLAND

Although there are tons of photo opps in Islands of Adventure, one of the coolest is your meeting with the master of webs, Spider-Man. You'll pose in front of a green screen and then you and Spidey will be digitally placed on the front of a Marvel magazine cover, complete with webs coming out of your hands. Look for this photo station inside the Marvel Alterniverse Store near the Spider-Man attraction.

Other neat meet-and-greet opportunites happen twice a day when some of your favorite Marvel characters appear across from The Amazing Adventures of Spider-Man. They'll take off dramatically on all-terrain three wheelers in a parade, then stop to meet fans, chat, and take pictures.

IT'S A
FACT

SECRET TRIBUTES INSIDE MARVEL SUPER HERO ISLAND

There are fun little details all around Marvel Super Hero Island. Usually, when you see someone's name in a sign, it is a special tribute. For instance, the sign "Nelson & Murdoch: Attorneys and Law" is a reference to Marvel's *Daredevil,* and the sign for "Blaze & Ketch mechanics" is a nod to *Ghost Rider.*

A TIP FOR MAJOR SPIDER-MAN FANS

Are you about to visit Universal's Islands of Adventure with a young Spider-Man fan? Have them call (407) 224-4001 before you go, and they'll hear a special message from their favorite web-slinger.

IT'S A
FACT

BEHIND THE AMAZING ADVENTURES OF SPIDER-MAN

The Amazing Adventures of Spider-Man is one of the most popular rides at Universal Orlando Resort. Here are some details you might not notice…

- There are incredible graphics in high-definition 3-D.

- There's a cameo appearance by Spider-Man co-creator Stan Lee.

- The audio system in each ride vehicle was upgraded from eight-channel to 16-channel surround sound to create a better experience for the rider.

- A new original music score featuring the beloved Spider-Man theme song, with a modern twist, was included in the 2012 upgrade.

- This ride covers 1.5 acres.

- The attraction simulates some incredible experiences, including a virtual 400-foot free fall.

- The attraction's design is the first ever to combine moving motion-based ride vehicles with 3-D film and live action.

A BUILDING OF A DIFFERENT COLOR

Have you ever noticed that the buildings inside Marvel Super Hero Island seem to change color as the day goes on?

This isn't superhero power at work, but it is a cool trick. Universal's designers used a special paint—called Chrome-Illusion—on the buildings to create this effect. This paint, which is sometimes used on cars, possesses three-sided crystals that produce different colors when the light and angles of view change.

IT'S A
FACT

INCREDIBLE HULK COASTER DETAILS

Here are some fun factoids you might not know about this beloved roller coaster...

- Its initial acceleration is zero to 40mph in just two seconds flat.

- You'll feel the rush as you fly through seven inversions, a 110-foot cobra roll, and two subterranean trenches.

- It reaches top speeds of 67mph.

- It takes so much power to launch The Incredible Hulk Coaster cars, Universal had to install on-site turbines to provide the launch, which happens every 20 seconds.

- A maximum number of 1,920 guests can ride this coaster each hour.

TOON LAGOON

Welcome to the colorful world of the Sunday comic strips. This is the island where Popeye, Dudley Do-Right, Family Circus, Broom-Hilda, Cathy, Beetle Bailey, Hagar the Horrible, Blondie, Betty Boop, and Marmaduke come to life. Toon Lagoon includes nods to more than 150 characters from 80 comic strips. Just like Marvel Super Hero Island, the theming here was challenging for the creative team to devise. The effort centered around showcasing the common features of these comic strips.

Overall, Toon Lagoon succeeds in providing a Sunday comic-strip feel. The three main attractions are Dudley Do-Right's Ripsaw Falls, Popeye & Bluto's Bilge-Rat Barges, and Me Ship, The Olive. But beware: The name Toon Lagoon is also a good indication of another essential ingredient in this land: water. This is the place to go if you're hot and need a good cooldown.

Dudley Do-Right's Ripsaw Falls

Well, it looks as though that notorious villain, Snidely Whiplash, has the lovable Nell in his clutches again, and it's up to Royal Canadian Mountie Dudley Do-Right to save her. This classic log-flume ride is a pretty safe bet for visitors who'd like to cool off and enjoy a cute, funny tale along the way. Get ready for the end of the ride when you'll take a watery plummet down Ripsaw Falls in a 75-foot drop.

Popeye & Bluto's Bilge-Rat Barges

While you're waiting in the queue for this ride, try saying Popeye & Bluto's Bilge-Rat Barges 10 times fast! Then, get ready to take an exciting, wet, white-water raft ride as Popeye tries to rescue Olive from Bluto. Water comes into your raft seemingly from every angle in this attraction, and you may even get sprayed from water cannons. If you really want a good soaking, this is the ride to for you.

Me Ship, The Olive

It's playtime for young visitors, the Popeye way. Kids will enjoy exploring this imaginative ship-themed play area, with interactive activities such as cargo nets for climbing, slides, horns, and even water cannons to shoot passengers riding Popeye & Bluto's Bilge-Rat Barges as they pass below.

Dining and Shopping in Toon Lagoon

For sit-down meals, Toon Lagoon offers three choices: Blondie's: Home of the Dagwood, Wimpy's, and the Comic Strip Cafe. Blondie's is themed after her husband, Dagwood, and his love of giant, overstuffed sandwiches. Popeye's buddy Wimpy has his own eatery, and, of course, you'll find hamburgers here as well as chicken fingers, chili dogs, fries, and more. Wimpy's has outdoor seating only. Last is the Comic Strip Cafe, a cafeteria-style dining option offering a slew of basic, though fairly unexciting, food choices, including fish and chips, hotdogs, burgers, and familiar Asian and Italian dishes. For a quick sweet treat, you can head to Cathy's Ice Cream stand, featuring Ben & Jerry's.

Toon Lagoon currently houses three stores for your shopping needs. For general Toon Lagoon merchandise, head to Toon Extra, which sells cartoon

character toys, including plush toys, apparel, DVDs, and more. Gasoline Alley is your destination for beach apparel and gear, such as beach towels, beach bags, sunglasses, hats, and T-shirts. Betty Boop fans haven't been forgotten in Toon Lagoon. Although this cartoon beauty doesn't have her own attraction, she does have her own store, where fans can buy all their Betty Boop T-shirts, mugs, dolls, collectible figurines, and more.

TACTICAL **TIP**

BUILT-IN STORAGE BINS

Since water tends to pour into your raft from
several directions when you're riding Popeye
& Bluto's Bilge-Rat Barges, Universal installed
plastic, covered bins in the center of each raft
to store personal items that shouldn't get wet.
Clever park visitors will place their shoes and
socks inside.

TACTICAL **TIP**

I'M SOAKED! WHERE CAN I GET A TOWEL?

If you find yourself soaking wet after an attraction and are in need of a towel, head to Gasoline Alley for beach towels. You can buy a new, and dry, T-shirt as well.

IT'S A FACT

ALL ABOUT DUDLEY DO-RIGHT'S RIPSAW FALLS

Here are some lesser-known facts about this popular water ride...

- This exciting, and wet, lagoon boat ride holds 400,000 gallons of water.

- The final flume drop is 75 feet, at a curved 55-degree angle.

- The end drop sends boats briefly below water level.

- This ride is considered an "aqua-coaster," which means it is half roller coaster, half flume ride.

IT'S A
FACT

WHAT SETS POPEYE & BLUTO'S BILGE-RAT BARGES APART?

When Universal Creative designed this attraction, they deviated from the typical rapids ride design. This is why the ride is special…

- The rafts speed up and slow down, unlike the typical ride that stays at one speed.

- There's more vertical (side to side, up and down) movement of the raft in the water, in what are called "super-elevations."

- The big, long lift at the end is filled with show elements to keep you more distracted (and wet) than is usually the case.

TACTICAL **TIP**

TAKE A PHOTO WITH MARMADUKE

There are seemingly countless photo opps around Toon Lagoon, but a fan favorite is the trick photography booth with Marmaduke. Head to Blondie's restaurant. The photo booth is outside and a sign shows how to set up this funny shot. You'll look like you're holding on for dear life as you "walk" Marmaduke.

Other great photo opps include standing under speech bubbles with quotes like, "It must be Sunday.... We're in Color!" and "I'm going to need a vacation from this vacation!"

IT'S A
FACT

FOLLOW THE
BLACK DOTTED LINES

Do those black dotted lines all around Toon Lagoon look familiar? If you take a moment to follow the dotted black lines spiraling all around the ground of King's Row in Toon Lagoon, you'll find they were left by Billy from the Family Circus. He's managed to escape his original comic strip bubble and has stepped into another one. These dotted black lines are a nod to the ones so often used in The Family Circus to show a character's travel path.

JURASSIC PARK

Step inside the island that was modeled after the *Jurassic Park* movie for an experience designed to mimic the famous flick. You'll enter a replica of the Jurassic Park gates and explore the exotic jungle environment filled with "dinosaurs." Watch out: Sometimes visitors come uncomfortably close to those giants of the earth. This island is also home to Camp Jurassic, Pteranodon Flyers, Jurassic Park River Adventure, and the Jurassic Park Discovery Center.

Camp Jurassic

Kids will have fun exploring this lush, prehistoric play area, including nets waiting to be climbed, Jurassic-themed slides, water cannons, caves, suspension bridges, and quarries to romp through. As Seuss Landing's If I Ran the Zoo play area appeals to young children, the 60,000-square-foot Camp Jurassic play area is a bit more attractive to older, preteens, though little ones will enjoy it too. This is a nice oasis for adults to enjoy some shade and catch their breath while kids run, climb, and play.

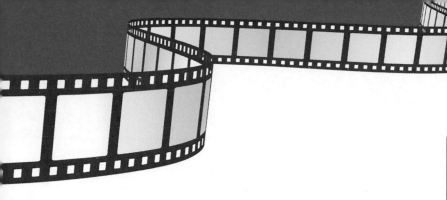

Pteranodon Flyers

Pteranodon Flyers is located inside Camp Jurassic, providing a chance to glide around the area and get a Pteranodon's-eye view. This ride is very specifically limited to children who are between 36 inches and 56 inches tall, with one supervising companion. The seats are designed one in front of the other, allowing for a nice view, but keep your child's personal limits in mind, in case he or she is afraid to sit alone.

A couple small thrills make this gliding ride extra fun, but overall it's pretty tame. Little ones flock to this attraction, so be prepared to wait awhile as the line can get long. The best time to try is first thing in the morning, or about an hour before the park closes.

Jurassic Park River Adventure

The Jurassic Park River Adventure attraction is the biggest draw for this island. This water ride starts off as a gentle tour of the fascinating dinosaurs now "living" in Jurassic Park. You'll pass by (slightly dated-looking) animatronic ultrasaurs, stegosaurs, and hydrosaurs. But then, as happens all too often, things go very wrong and your boat ends up in the raptor containment unit (where the raptors are not contained).

Your boat is then sent into the Enviromental Systems building to save you, but you aren't out of danger yet. Raptors are still after you and your only escape is straight toward a giant, very scary T-Rex. Just as you reach him, you'll plunge down a heart-stopping 85-foot drop into the waters below. There's enough going on just before the plunge that you don't really have time to prepare yourself; the effect is fantastic.

Jurassic Park Discovery Center

The Jurassic Park Discovery Center is a great place to get out of the heat with the kids and enjoy hands-on exhibits that are part science and part fantasy. You'll get to see a huge T-Rex skeleton, visit a nursery housing dinosaur eggs, see a baby velociraptor hatch from its shell, engage in a quiz-show game experience, see fossilized dinosaur fragments, and view the world from a dinosaur's perspective through high-tech viewfinders. It may be tricky explaining what's real and what's fantasy to young kids, but it's still an enjoyable time.

Dining and Shopping in Jurassic Park

Inside Jurassic Park, you'll have your pick from four dining options: the Pizza Predattoria, The Burger Digs, Thunder Falls Terrace, and The Watering Hole. Pizza Predattoria is an outdoor walk-up window pizza stand, specializing in personal-sized pizzas, meatball subs, and chicken Caesar salads. At The Burger Digs, you can take a break with some indoor air-conditioning in this quick-service eatery, serving up burgers, veggie burgers, chicken sandwiches, chicken tenders, and more. Thunder Falls Terrace is an indoor cafeteria-style restaurant, offering a tasty array of barbeque ribs, wraps, smoked turkey legs, rotisserie chicken, and more. Last is The Watering Hole outdoor walk-up window stand, offering cocktails, beer, wine, frozen beverages, chili, nachos, hotdogs, and even wings.

There are just two spots to shop in Jurassic Park. First up is the aptly named Dinostore, where, as you can guess, you'll find everything dinosaur lovers might want. Inside, you'll find books, apparel, toys, and even fossil replicas. The second shopping option is Jurassic Outfitters, which offers Jurassic Park apparel, toys, adventure gear, and more. This store also stocks towels in case you've received a bigger soaking than you planned on the Jurassic Park River Adventure.

ENJOYABLE EXTRAS AT CAMP JURASSIC

If you'd like to give your little ones a thrill, take them for a walk along the Thunder Lizard Trail. As they follow the prehistoric footprints on the path, the ground will rumble with the roar of dinosaurs.

Another fun activitiy for kids is looking for dinosaur eggs hidden in the vegetation around Jurassic Park.

IT'S A
FACT

BIG RIVER

Can you guess how many gallons of water are used in the Jurassic Park River Adventure attraction? This exciting water ride requires a whopping 1.5-million gallons of water.

Here's another cool fact about this ride: When it was built, the 85-foot plunge you take at the end was the largest theme park water descent ever constructed.

TACTICAL **TIPS**

SCENIC VIEW

If you're looking for a scenic spot in the park, go out the back door of Jurassic Park Discovery Center. It opens onto a terrace presenting a lovely view of Islands of Adventure.

VIEW OF THE PARK

If you'd like to watch other park visitors take the 85-foot plunge at the end of Jurassic Park River Adventure while you grab a bite to eat, try Thunder Falls Terrace (named for a reason!). There are windows overlooking the River Adventure falls, along with outdoor seating that takes in the exciting view as well.

FAN FACT

Only fans of the first *Jurassic Park* movie will know why there's a Barbasol shaving cream can sitting inside the Jurassic Park Discovery Center. This nod to the original movie is related to the high-tech storage device devised to look like a Barbasol shaving cream can; it was used by actor Dennis Nedry when he stole dinosaur eggs.

IT'S A
FACT

HOW MUCH SPACE DO DINOSAURS NEED?

Jurassic Park is the largest island at Universal's Islands of Adventure, occupying an expansive 21 acres. (The Wizarding World of Harry Potter – Hogsmeade comes in a close second at 20 acres.) That's equivalent to the size of approximately 15 football fields.

THE LOST CONTINENT

Although some of this area's magic has been lost since its neighbor The Wizarding World of Harry Potter – Hogsmeade moved in, The Lost Continent still has a wonderful atmosphere. You'll see giant pieces of an "ancient" Poseidon statue, including his famous trident. Nearby you might notice carvings of titans in an extinct volcano. The look of this area is worth a peek, even you aren't stopping for the attractions. (Rumor has it that The Lost Continent may be replaced sometime in the near future, but there was no official announcement at the time this book went to press.) You can catch The Eighth Voyage of Sindbad Stunt Show here as well as Poseidon's Fury. The talking Mystic Fountain, which was originally a feature to be discovered as a surprise, is now listed on Universal's Map as an attraction here as well.

The Eighth Voyage of Sindbad Stunt Show

Watch legendary hero Sindbad and his sidekick Kabob navigate their way through an adventure where they're sure to find danger and excitement. Sindbad must rescue the lovely Princess Amora from the evil clutches of sorceress Miseria by recovering the precious Sultan's Heart Ruby. Of course, there are many obstacles to overcome along the way; one nice, modern twist is that Princess Amora is an empowered girl, aiding Sindbad instead of being the typical helpless princess we all know from older stories. This show also has an abundance of slapstick comedy infused with impressive stunts, water explosions, and lots of pyrotechnic effects.

Poseidon's Fury

This walk-through special effects attraction centers around Poseidon's battle with enemy Lord Darkenon. Be sure to stop for a moment to appreciate the look of the attraction entrance: the broken, gigantic pieces of Poseidon's statue, the once beautiful but now damaged mosaic floor, and more. Once inside, you'll eventually encounter an assistant named Taylor, who explains that archeologist Professor Baxter and his company have vanished. She takes you on a tour of this old damaged structure, which was once a temple to Poseidon. But, as you can guess, things go horribly wrong—you are trapped below in the middle of a battle between Poseidon (enter water effects) and Lord Darkenon (cue pyrotechnic effects). Universal doesn't hold back the special effects here.

Mystic Fountain

The Mystic Fountain was originally a special surprise for folks nearby the entrance of The Eighth Voyage of Sindbad Stunt Show, but Universal has now included it on the Islands of Adventure map as its own attraction. At first glance, The Mystic Fountain just seems like another attractive detail that is part of The Lost Continent. Once you visit, though, you'll find this fountain has a "spirit" inside, who speaks, cracks jokes, and asks riddles. And beware: The spirit's main intention is to get you wet in any way it can. Kids will especially love this quick, entertaining experience.

Dining and Shopping in The Lost Continent

Dining in The Lost Continent is centered around the highly acclaimed Mythos Restaurant. Considered by many folks to be one of the best amusement park restaurants in the world, Mythos is modeled to look like the inside of a volcano that has been hollowed out by the gods themselves. There's also a beautiful outdoor seating area with a scenic view of the inland sea. Mythos couples lovely ambience with award-winning contemporary cuisine, including seared salmon, mahi mahi, and beef medallions. Reservations are accepted, and are recommended in this family-friendly restaurant, especially during busy seasons. But even if you're not planning on eating at Mythos, it's still worth taking a quick peek inside.

The Lost Continent also features two fast-food stands: the Fire Eaters Grill and Doc Sugrue's Desert Kebab House. At the Fire Eaters Grill you can grab quicker options, such as hotdogs, salads, gyros, and Fiery Chicken Stingers. Or, you can head over to Doc Sugrue's Desert Kebab House for chicken, beef, and veggie kebabs, along with salads, yogurt, churros, and more.

Shopping in The Lost Continent offers up a more unique array of merchandise to bring home than some of the other islands. Treasures of Poseidon features sea-inspired T-shirts, sandals, handbags, and jewelry. You can take in the wide array of Japanese cultured pearls at The Pearl Factory. Merchandise ranges from modest to very expensive here; you can select an unopened oyster and discover a pearl within. The Coin Mint is the spot to purchase one-of-a-kind medallions and coins, forged and created right in front of you. Historic Families – Heraldry displays lovely family coat of arms merchandise as well as an armory of historic swords and daggers. Finally, Star Souls offers psychic readings and temporary henna body art.

IT'S A
FACT

BEHIND POSEIDON'S FURY

In order to create the exciting experience of Poseidon's Fury, Universal designed more than 200 individual special effects, including 25-foot fireballs, four types of lasers, water cannons, mist screens, and water mortars. An amazing 350,000 gallons of water are used during each show.

THE EIGHTH VOYAGE OF SINDBAD

Spoiler Alert! At the end of The Eighth Voyage of Sindbad, the audience is treated to a "Flaming High Dive" stunt, where the stunt performer is set on fire and then falls 22 feet into a watery pit.

IT'S A **FACT**

MAKING ROOM FOR HARRY

Did you know that part of The Lost Continent was removed for the installation of The Wizarding World of Harry Potter – Hogsmeade? The Lost Continent section, formerly dedicated to Merlin, was utilized for Hogsmeade, leaving The Lost Continent smaller though still worth a visit—especially for the architectural theming and Mythos Restaurant.

IT'S A
FACT

DO YOUR OWN STUNTS

Dreaming of becoming a stunt man or woman like the ones in The Eighth Voyage of Sindbad? The performers who work in this attraction have to go through a rigorous audition, including obstacle courses; swimming, strength and agility tests; executing specific stunts; and acting.

IT'S A FACT

LOST FROM THE THE LOST CONTINENT

First-time visitors to the park may not know that the Dragon Challenge roller coaster inside The Wizarding World of Harry Potter – Hogsmeade was originally part of The Lost Continent and was called Dueling Dragons. Universal Creative made some Harry Potter-style modifications and repurposed the attraction.

SEUSS LANDING

"From there to here, and here to there, funny things are everywhere!" wrote Dr. Seuss. There is hardly a visitor who comes through the Islands of Adventure gates that isn't familiar with Dr. Seuss' beloved children's books and the lovable, wacky world within. Universal did the job right, though, with incredible theming that allows visitors to feel as though they magically landed inside a favorite Dr. Seuss book.

Nearly every architectural line has been painstakingly designed to be curved or crooked, just like the books. It's difficult to find a single straight line or 90-degree angle throughout Seuss Landing. Even the landscaping matches the wacky atmosphere here, and this land's color scheme replicates Dr. Seuss' illustrations perfectly. Even if you're not planning on riding anything here, it's certainly worth a stroll through just to see the place. It's a work of art.

The High in the Sky Seuss Trolley Train Ride

All aboard this sweet trolley train ride, which provides a bird's-eye view of Seuss Landing. As you move through the queue, you'll learn all about the story of the Sneetches, featuring Sylvester McMonkey McBean. This ride has a duel track: One part continues the story of the Sneetches, and the second takes you through the ABCs of Seuss Landing. Also note that one of the tracks will take you around the inside of the Circus McGurkus Cafe Stoo-pendous.

Caro-Seuss-el

The Caro-Seuss-el is a beautifully created Dr. Seuss version of the classic carousel ride. The little details here are worth a look even if you don't ride. Instead of the classic horses, the Caro-Seuss-el is filled with 54 marvelous creatures from Dr. Seuss books, such as twin camels from *One Fish, Two Fish, Red Fish, Blue Fish*, elephant birds from *Horton Hatches the Egg*, and cowfish from *McElligot's Pool*. Of course, there are no straight lines here; not even the poles mounting the animals are straight. To make the ride even more enjoyable, these creatures are interactive. Pull on the reins or push the lever on the neck to see your creature turn its head turn, blink its eyes, or wiggle its ears.

One Fish, Two Fish, Red Fish, Blue Fish

This sweet, classic ride has been given a little twist Dr. Seuss-style. Kids get to ride in a circular motion in fish that look like they're out of the *One Fish, Two Fish, Red Fish, Blue Fish* book. The twist comes in the form of a squirt: The ride plays a song, and if you don't listen to the words and do what the song tell you, you'll get squirted. This adds some excitement and, of course, a chance to get sprayed—which is always a good thing on a hot day.

The Cat in the Hat

"It is fun to have fun, but you have to know how," said Dr. Seuss' beloved character. You and your family will love this re-creation of the Cat in the Hat story. You'll board your six-person "couch" vehicle, which takes you through 18 scenes of the Cat in the Hat's crazy afternoon with Thing One™ and Thing Two™ and, of course, the Fish who continues to protest of the mess happening all around him. This is a dark ride, similar to E.T., and expect some twists and turns—even a couple of 360-degree spins. The scenes are colorful and full of fun with animated sculptures and great visual stimulation. Very young children are not always happy with the zippy movements of this ride.

If I Ran the Zoo

Step inside young Gerald McGrew's idea of what a zoo should be. This is a wonderful interactive play area for little kids. Charming, unusual Dr. Seuss creatures appear from behind hedges when you step on a pedal, turn a crank, or tickle their feet. Slide down the tunnels of Zomba-matant and even crawl through a cave in Kartoom. Of course, there's a wet play area as well, where you can trap beasts (or a friend) in a cage made of water. You can also visit Scrabble Foot Mulligatawny, but watch out or he'll sneeze on you. There's so much here to enjoy, and it's a great place to catch your breath while your kids let out some energy and get a break from waiting in all those attraction lines.

Dining and Shopping in Seuss Landing

When it's time to eat in Seuss Landing, you have four options. For quick-service sit-down dining, select Circus McGurkus Cafe Stoo-pendous. You also have three walk-up window options: the Green Eggs and Ham Cafe, Hop on Pop Ice Cream Shop, and Moose Juice, Goose Juice.

Head inside the big top Circus McGurkus Cafe Stoo-pendous for fried chicken, spaghetti, pizza, cheeseburgers, and more. Kids will enjoy waving to travelers on the The High in the Sky Seuss Trolley Train Ride as the trolley track circles around the inside of the building.

What would a visit to the world of Dr. Seuss be without trying Green Eggs and Ham? You actually can get a special Green Eggs and Ham sandwich at the Green Eggs and Ham Cafe. Other options at this dining spot include hamburgers and chicken fingers.

Just look for the stand shaped like giant piece of green ham. At the Hop on Pop Ice Cream Shop, you'll find an array of cool treats, such as root beer floats, waffle cones, and ice cream sundaes. Lastly, at the Moose Juice, Goose Juice you can order fresh fruit cups, smoothies, juices, pretzels, cookies, and more.

If you'd like to do some shopping in Seuss Landing, there are four stores. Cats, Hats & Things offers an array of merchandise, such as apparel and toys featuring the beloved cat and his companions, including Thing One and Thing Two. All The Books You Can Read offers some of your favorite Dr. Seuss books, along with apparel, toys, and DVDs. Snookers & Snookers Sweet Candy Cookers is your destination for homemade fudge, cotton candy, caramel apples, and more. The Mulberry Street Store is the biggest shop in Seuss Landing, covering the widest array of Dr. Seuss merchandise, including an abundance of apparel, toys, mugs, hats, wigs, CDs, DVDs, books, games, and much more.

SEUSS LANDING ZAX BYPASS

If you stroll by the Zax ByPass and can't quite place the two yellow characters seemingly in a standoff or argument, here's the scoop. These guys are the North-Going and South-Going Zax from *The Sneetches and Other Stories*. The characters meet each other as they are walking northward and southward, and each refuses to move for the other to pass. Their incredibly long standoff continues while the world grows and develops all around them, the way it does here in Seuss Landing. You'll see the Seuss Trolley tracks above as well as shops and restaurants built encircling them.

TACTICAL **TIP**

FANTASTIC PHOTO OPPS IN SEUSS LANDING

You'll get some great photo opportunities with the famous Dr. Seuss characters who roam Seuss Landing. Take a picture with the Cat in the Hat, Thing One or Thing Two, or even the Grinch™.

There's also a nice photo opp behind Circus McGurkus, featuring a colorful egg in a nest. This is the egg from *Horton Hatches the Egg*, in which Horton promises to sit on the egg, prompting such excitement that Horton, the nest, and even the tree are moved to the circus. Climb on top of the egg (the sign encourages visitors to do so) for a memorable photo.

IT'S A FACT

SEUSS FROM THE SOURCE

Did you know part of the vision for Seuss Landing came from Dr. Seuss' wife, Audrey Geisel? Theodore Geisel (aka "Dr. Seuss") passed away in 1991, and his wife holds the rights to his creations. When Universal arranged with her for the right to install Seuss Landing, the company agreed to meet some of her requirements about theming. She wanted visitors to feel they were stepping inside Dr. Seuss books, so the island needed to look and feel the part.

Another part of the agreement when Universal obtained rights to create Seuss Landing is that the land will never participate in Universal's well-known Halloween Horror Nights.

SHH... IT'S A SECRET

HEAR THE LORAX™ STORY AT THE ONCE-LER'S HOUSE

If you head over to the Once-ler's house in Seuss Landing, be sure to lean into the end of the silly, twisting pipes with a spout at the end, where there's a little sign that says, "Listen." You'll be able to hear the Lorax's story. Lorax fans will also surely notice the Truffula™ trees growing nearby.

Universal's Islands of Adventure

WHAT IS MCELLIGOT'S POOL?

Wondering what "McElligot's Pool"—the little fish pond by the entrance to Seuss Landing—refers too? This is a nod to the Dr. Seuss book *McElligot's Pool*, in which a young boy named Marco dreams about all the wonderful fish in his small pond.

IT'S A
FACT

SEUSS LANDING'S WACKY TREES

The wavy, curvy palm trees inside Seuss Landing were actually made into those crazy shapes by nature. These palms were damaged during Hurricane Andrew, forcing them into their current shapes. It was decided that Universal would relocate them into Seuss Landing because they fit so well into the island's ethos.

IT'S A
FACT

WELCOME TO SNEETCH BEACH

Did you know Seuss Landing dedicated its waterfront section to Sneetches? Situated behind the Green Eggs and Ham Cafe, this little area is called Sneetch Beach. You'll see some Sneetches in the water, and catch some great views of the park while you're there.

TACTICAL **TIP**

ADVICE FROM DR. SEUSS

If your children are upset when it's time to leave Seuss Landing, try consoling them with some advice from Dr. Seuss himself: "Don't cry because it's over, smile because it happened." (It also may help to buy a small treat or a Cat in the Hat chapeau on the way out.)

SHH... IT'S A SECRET
ORLANDO
FLORIDA

CREATING SEUSS LANDING

To create the wacky, curvy lines in Seuss
Landing, one of the architectural design
tricks was the use of special, hand-sculpted
expanded polystyrene foam. This material also
allowed paint colors to appear quite vibrant,
which was needed to create the theming
for Seuss Landing. Universal Creative was
concerned about how well this material would
hold up to the harsh weather conditions of
Orlando, so they placed some test material in
the area that would eventually become Seuss
Landing for six months to see how robust it
was. Needless to say, it held up.

CHAPTER THREE

THE WIZARDING WORLD OF HARRY POTTER

WHEN UNIVERSAL WON THE RIGHTS to incorporate the incredibly popular Harry Potter series into its theme parks, the move helped solidify the resort as a major destination in Florida. Author J.K. Rowling was given a great deal of artistic control over its development, which has certainly enhanced fans' experiences and aided in making The Wizarding World of Harry Potter a screaming success. The theming in Hogsmeade and Diagon Alley is extraordinary, leading to a new level of theme-park immersion. Since the opening of Hogsmeade, in June 2010, and then the addition of Diagon Alley, in July 2014, the parks' attendance rates have soared.

This chapter is solely dedicated to The Wizarding World of Harry Pottter as a whole, even though the two sections—Hogsmeade and Diagon Alley—are actually located in two separate parks.

HOGSMEADE

Harry Potter experts were part of the design team and that is just one of the reasons The Wizarding World of Harry Potter – Hogsmeade is such a success today. The village of Hogsmeade was designed by Universal Creative with consultation from author J.K. Rowling, herself, as well as Harry Potter film production designer, Stuart Craig. The collaboration certainly paid off.

Hogsmeade's re-creation at Universal's Islands of Adventure gives fans a chance to step inside and explore for themselves the only village solely inhabited by magical beings. In the Harry Potter stories, Hogsmeade is set in Scotland and was founded by the famous wizard Hengist of Woodcroft, who was fleeing Muggle persecution. In the novels, Hogwarts students are allowed to visit the more than 1,000-year-old village after they enter their third year of wizarding school, and then only with permission from their guardians.

The comprehensive design of Hogsmeade helps visitors immerse themselves in Harry's world, down to the quirky cobblestone streets (warning for those with difficulty walking: the ground here is a bit uneven), snow-capped eaves, and intentionally congested rows of storefronts full of magical items. Serious Harry Potter fans can spend hours exploring the facades and inside the actual shops.

In terms of attractions, Hogsmeade offers Harry Potter and the Forbidden Journey, which is inside Hogwarts Castle; the Dragon Challenge; Flight of the Hippogriff; and Ollivanders wand shop/show.

Dragon Challenge

If you love roller coasters, this may be two minutes and 45 seconds you won't forget. The Dragon Challenge is actually two different, intertwined high-speed roller coasters in one. You'll fly with either the Chinese Fireball or the Hungarian Horntail. These coasters are both inverted, which means the ride track is above the passenger cars, leaving riders' feet dangling. The cars have been designed to look like dragons clutching the screeching riders with their claws. This twisting, stomach-churning ride includes some near misses, but not with the coaster on the alternate track.

Harry Potter and the Forbidden Journey

Get ready for an intense, action-packed ride that you could only experience in the world of Harry Potter. Before you even enter this structure—designed to represent Hogwarts Castle—take a moment to appreciate the level of detail that Universal put into this impressive Harry Potter eye candy. Folks who do not wish to ride Forbidden Journey can still check out this remarkable "tour" of Hogwarts and take a special exit before the ride's boarding area. There's a separate "castle tour only" line, (which does not, unfortunately, include the dungeon).

The line, or "Hogwarts tour," begins in the dungeon; it includes the potions classroom and passes into the greenhouse before entering the castle corridors. It's here that you'll see astounding portraits that seem to be true oil paintings, though they move and even speak, just as they do in the best-selling novels. Next up is Headmaster Dumbledore's office,

followed by the Defense Against the Dark Arts classroom, and finally the Gryffindor common room, where you'll be prepared to board the "enchanted benches" for your adventure. There are so many Potter-esque details on view in the queue area, you can go through it several times and still see something new.

Warning: for those prone to motion sickness, this isn't a straight-up simulator ride, and you may feel queasy as you exit. If you can handle it, though, it's worth the risk—especially if you're a die-hard Harry Potter fan.

You'll go on a head-spinning journey with Harry, Ron, and Hermione. The story is a little weak and chaotic as it attempts to include many of the novels' "greatest hits," and the graphics aren't quite as impressive as the Terminator 2: 3-D attraction, but the effects and incredible sense of motion more than make up for it. Potter fans are usually able to forgive these small shortcomings of this attraction.

Flight of the Hippogriff

The Flight of the Hippogriff is a more family-friendly junior coaster focused on Hagrid and his class devoted to the Care of Magical Creatures. You're urged to follow Hagrid's instructions on how to approach the animatronic Hippogriff, Buckbeak™ (a magical creature with the head of an eagle and the body of a horse), as you pass him perched in his nest. You'll board the Hippogriff's car for a coaster ride swooping through Hagrid's pumpkin patch and past his stone hut. Great views of Hogsmeade and Hogwarts Castle are available from this ride. Note: smaller children and those who prefer a gentler ride will be happier in the front row of the coaster car, while thrill-seekers should head for the back rows.

Outdoor Stage Shows at Hogsmeade

There are two unscheduled shows that rotate on the small stage area in Hogsmeade. One is the Frog Choir, where you'll listen to some modernized Harry Potter songs sung by Hogwarts student singers along with their (puppet) frog companions. The second performance is the Triwizard Spirit Rally, where students from Beauxbatons Academy of Magic and Durmstrang Institute perform for the crowd and pose for photos.

Dining and Shopping in Hogsmeade

If you're dining in Hogsmeade, Three Broomsticks offers a British-style menu, including fish and chips, corn pasties, and shepherd's pie. There are also a few American options like rotisserie chicken and ribs. Next door is the Hog's Head pub for Butterbeer™, actual beer, and mixed drinks.

Shopping in Hogsmeade, as well as in Diagon Alley, feels like an attraction in and of itself. There are seemingly endless choices of Harry Potter treasures to choose from. There are replica wands, Hogwarts robes, Bertie Bott's Every Flavour Beans™, and Chocolate Frogs™. It will be hard for any true Harry Potter fan to hold back.

Dervish and Banges is a perfect spot for new wizards and witches in search of school supplies. You'll find a large array of Hogwarts-related items, such as class robes, scarves, house neckties,

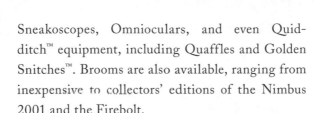

Sneakoscopes, Omnioculars, and even Quidditch™ equipment, including Quaffles and Golden Snitches™. Brooms are also available, ranging from inexpensive to collectors' editions of the Nimbus 2001 and the Firebolt.

Filch's Emporium of Confiscated Goods is located at the exit of the Forbidden Journey attraction. There are several "confiscated" props to view and plenty of Hogwarts merchandise available, such as hats, T-shirts, and stationery. There are also wizard chess sets, swords, and magical creature toys. You don't need to ride Harry Potter and the Forbidden Journey to shop at Filch's. Look for the shop entrance between the castle entrance and the Flight of the Hippogriff.

Honeydukes is a colorful candy shop that sells all the cool Harry Potter treats you've always wanted to try. Here's the spot to buy Chocolate Frogs, Bertie Bott's Every-Flavour Beans, Fizzing Whizzbees, Exploding Bonbons, and much, much more.

Ollivanders, as more thoroughly explained later in this chapter, is the number-one place to get your wizardly wand. You can purchase the original collector's series as well as the interactive series. Both lines offer a variety of wands to choose from, including wand replicas of your favorite Harry Potter characters. The number of styles available for the interactive wands is smaller, but Universal seems to keep expanding these as they are wildly popular. You can also check out the cool wand show running in a room next door. For more details, see "Ollivanders" in the "Hogsmeade and Diagon Alley" section in this book. Lastly, the Owl Post—adjacent to Ollivanders—is where you'll find Harry Potter stationery, stamps, writing implements, and, of course, a variety of owl-themed toys and gifts.

HOGWARTS CASTLE:
VIRTUALLY ENORMOUS

Ever marvel at how huge Hogwarts Castle looks?
Engineers designed the castle using a trick called
forced perspective, which makes objects seem
bigger than they are. The ground floor of the
building is designed at a normal size and each
additional story is then built using a smaller scale
than the previous floor. This makes the castle look
much bigger, similar to how a large structure
would look from a distance. Many theme parks
employ this cool trick.

IT'S A
FACT

THE DRAGON CHALLENGE

Previous visitors may remember that the Dragon Challenge dual roller coaster was originally called Dueling Dragons and was part of The Lost Continent island. The ride was repurposed for The Wizarding World of Harry Potter – Hogsmeade in reference to the Triwizard Tournament from *Harry Potter and the Goblet of Fire*. The fact this attraction wasn't specifically built for Hogsmeade may be one of the reasons lines for this ride aren't always incredibly long.

In its earliest iteration, the ride included several near-miss experiences between the two intertwined coasters. In 2011, Universal removed the simulated near-misses due to some rider injuries caused by flying objects.

RIDING THE ROBOCOASTER

Did you know that the "enchanted bench" you ride inside Harry Potter and the Forbidden Journey attraction is actually a complicated ride system employing robocoaster robotic arms?

The benches are mounted to the ride track above them by rotating robotic arms, which offer motion in any direction. They have the ability to take riders upside down and even spin, but those capabilities are not employed in this ride.

IT'S A
FACT

FLIGHT OF THE HIPPOGRIFF

Check out these facts about The Flight of the Hippogriff…

- The Flight of the Hippogriff was originally the Flying Unicorn attraction from The Lost Continent, but was repurposed for The Wizarding World of Harry Potter – Hogsmeade. When the ride was revamped for Hogsmeade, some of the additions included a replica of Hagrid's hut and the animatronic Hippogriff, Buckbeak.

- The coaster takes you up to speeds of 28mph along a 1,000-foot track.

- This coaster track was designed and built by Vekoma, and the same model track is found on the Barnstormer coaster at Walt Disney World.

- If you compare Flight of the Hippogriff to Universal Orlando Resort's Woody Woodpecker's Nuthouse Coaster, the Flight of the Hippogriff is 7mph faster and 400 feet longer.

HOGWARTS CASTLE

If you're traveling with a serious Harry Potter fan, keep your eyes peeled for the original sword of Gryffindor. It is on display in Dumbledore's office.

MOANING MYRTLE IN HOGSMEADE

Keep yours ears open when you enter the public bathrooms in Hogsmeade. You'll hear Moaning Myrtle's complaints and cries.

TACTICAL **TIP**

MAIL A LETTER FROM HOGSMEADE

If you'd like to send a neat memento to a friend at home, stop by the Owl Post Station near the Owl Post store. You can mail letters here and they'll arrive with an official Hogsmeade stamp on the envelope. You can purchase some stationery in the Owl Post or bring your own letter with you. (You pay for postage.)

SHH... IT'S A SECRET

ORLANDO
FLORIDA

DERVISH AND BANGES

Before you leave Dervish and Banges, be
sure to check out the caged *Monster Book of
Monsters*, which was featured in *Harry Potter
and the Prisoner of Azkaban*. But beware, it
bites (not really).

SHARED ATTRACTIONS IN HOGSMEADE AND DIAGON ALLEY

Although Hogsmeade and Diagon Alley are in two different amusement parks, they share a few things in common—most notably the Hogwarts Express train, which runs back and forth between them. This section covers the features that Hogsmeade and Diagon Alley share.

Ollivanders

You can visit Ollivanders wand shop in both Hogsmeade and Diagon Alley. Harry Potter fans will recall that Ollivanders was the wand shop in Diagon Alley where Harry bought his wand. In fact, in the Harry Potter series, your wand chooses you, not the other way around. Universal made sure to incorporate this magical experience into its parks with a "show" inside both Ollivanders shops in Hogsmeade and Diagon Alley. Of course, you can purchase a wand of your own choosing in either of these shops as well.

These stores are filled with many types of wands, including some that are replicas of your favorite characters'. There are still more types to choose from, including birthday wands and collectible sets.

Ollivanders Wand Chooses the Wizard Show

Ollivanders offers another cool "attraction" though it isn't marked on the Islands of Adventure map and there aren't even signs outside the door. If you want to experience the Wand Chooses the Wizard show, you'll have to wait in line (doors are not really marked, but look for the chain barriers and an attendant next to the main entrance of the store). Ollivanders only admits 15 to 20 people per session, so you may wait awhile if the line is long.

Inside, a wand keeper will select someone from the group (usually a child), and then go through the process of matching the person to the proper wand. Incorrectly matched wands create mishaps, such as shelves that collapse, and the correct match only becomes obvious when some wonderful magic happens. The special effects employed in this show are relatively simple, but it's great fun—even for those who are not selected. This is a must-see for Potter fans.

Interactive Wands

Like the Wand Chooses the Wizard show, this isn't an official attraction in and of itself, but the Interactive Wands available at The Wizarding World of Harry Potter deserve a mention. Just as you can purchase the standard collectors wands in all the shops, you can also buy interactive wands that come with a special map. Once you obtain your wand, check out your map and head out into the streets of either Diagon Alley or Hogsmeade. You'll spot gold medallions imbedded in the ground. Follow the pattern on the medallion with your wand, say the proper incantation, and wait for something very magical to happen in the store window in front of you.

The Hogwarts Express

Universal broke new ground in creating this unique but quite appropriate way to connect the two Wizarding Worlds of Harry Potter with a transportation method that's also an attraction. In order to ride the Hogwarts Express you'll need a park-to-park pass along with your regular admission ticket. The Hogwarts Express runs from London's King's Cross Station, located next to Diagon Alley, to Hogsmeade Station, and back. Each direction offers a different, enchanting experience onboard.

King's Cross Station is a well-crafted replica of the real King's Cross station in London, complete with British "Muggle" train station attendants...until you cross into Platform 9¾, where you'll then encounter Hogwarts Express conductors.

TACTICAL **TIP**

INTERACTIVE WANDS

Some of the interactive wand areas are harder to trigger than others and may require the user to make several attempts. Here are a couple of tips…

- Try to cast the spell motion using just your wrist and not your whole arm. (It's not as much fun, but this usually provides greater success.)

- Try to direct the motion of your wand directly toward the four red lights in the window (at the hidden motion-sensitive camera).

- It isn't necessary to say the accompanying incantation, but you'll probably want to anyway.

- If you're still having trouble casting your spell, look for wand attendants who are usually on hand to help. They can actually make the experience more enjoyable, as they will assist you in character.

HOGWARTS EXPRESS: SPOILER ALERT

As you start your passage from the London side of King's Cross Station to Platform 9¾, be sure to look to your left at the passengers ahead of you. You'll watch them disappear into the wall just like Harry does in the movie. Then, you'll get your turn to disappear as you walk around the corner into a corridor. Trick mirrors create the illusion of your own disappearance to the amazement of passengers behind you.

SHH... IT'S A SECRET
ORLANDO FLORIDA

WHERE TO CAST YOUR SPELL

Did you know Universal included some secret interactive locations to use a wand in The Wizarding World of Harry Potter? There are a couple ways to locate them. Have your young wand owner ask a "wand attendant" about them, or keep a sharp eye out for motion-sensor cameras (look for four red dots of light) carefully placed in shop windows. The wand attendants usually stand outside nearby the wand instructional medallions in the ground. One such secret location is in the Scribbulus Writing Implements store window. Another spot is the faux storefront of Slug and Jiggers Apothecary.

TACTICAL **TIPS**

BUTTERBEER: A MUST DRINK

Any Harry Potter fan will be familiar with the famous beverage, Butterbeer. You can try one for yourself inside either Hogsmeade or Diagon Alley at many of the restaurants and food stands. The biggest debate isn't whether Butterbeer is tasty; it seems to be whether the regular, hot, or frozen style is best.

OLLIVANDERS WAND SHOP

The Ollivanders wand shop's Wand Chooses the Wizard show in Diagon Alley often offers a shorter wait than the the identical show in Hogsmeade. This is because the shop in Diagon Alley has multiple rooms offering the wand selection experience. The Ollivanders in Hogsmeade has just one wand-selection room.

HOGWARTS EXPRESS:
SPOILER ALERT

Aboard the Hogwarts Express, you'll experience much more than a simple train ride with views of the park. You'll be escorted into a train car just like the ones Harry and his classmates ride in and enjoy views of London and the Scottish countryside, including some magical moments. Be sure to turn and look at your door when you hear familiar voices. You'll see silhouettes and sound effects of some of your favorite Harry Potter characters.

The Wizarding World of Harry Potter

INTERACTIVE WAND MAPS: SPOILER ALERT

To make things even more exciting, Universal has included some "invisible" messages on the interactive wand maps. Head for the dark and spooky Knockturn Alley, where certain areas will illuminate the secret messages.

TACTICAL **TIP**

OLLIVANDERS WAND CHOOSES THE WIZARD SHOW

If you have more than one wizard or witch who's hoping to be chosen for the Wand Chooses the Wizard show, you can hope that the Wand Keeper allows two wand seekers to participate. (This happens sometimes.) You can discreetly ask the attendant or gently motion to the Wand Keeper as the show starts. Sometimes they are willing to accommodate you.

DIAGON ALLEY

In the Harry Potter series, Diagon Alley is a secret, magical-beings-only shopping district in London—accessible only from the Leaky Cauldron. Gringotts Bank is stationed there, too, along with a fascinating collection of magical shops and restaurants. Students often frequent Diagon Alley to purchase school supplies, as did Harry, when he was accompanied there by Hagrid in *Harry Potter and the Sorcerer's Stone.*

At Universal, Diagon Alley's entrance isn't through the back of the Leaky Cauldron, (although you can visit this famous establishment once inside) but instead via an unmarked entrance on the front of the London facade, right next to King's Cross Station.

Be sure to pause in front of the London frontage before entering Diagon Alley for a moment to study the apartment building, which includes a replica of Sirius Black's residence, 12 Grimmauld Place, as well as a replica of the Fountain of Eros. King's Cross Station is also located in "London," where you can board the Hogwarts Express.

Inside Diagon Alley, there's a tremendous amount of eye candy for Harry Potter fans to take in. You can check out Gringotts Bank and ride the Escape from Gringotts attraction, visit Ollivanders wand shop (and the Wand Chooses the Wizard show), stroll through a slew of magical shops, try Butterbeer, play with your new interactive wand, eat at the Leaky Cauldron, and dine at several other non-Muggle eateries. There are also two outdoor shows that run on the stage by Carkitt Market, one featuring Celestina Warbeck and the Banshees, and the second, a retelling of *The Tales of Beedle the Bard*.

Harry Potter and the Escape from Gringotts

Get ready for a wild adventure as you're swept up into the story of Harry, Ron, and Hermione's escape from Gringotts Bank, from *Harry Potter and the Deathly Hallows*. In this attraction, you are opening an account and receiving a tour on the same day of Harry's visit. Of course, your tour goes terribly wrong when it's assumed you are part of the kids' villainous break-in.

Your line moves through the Great Hall of the bank, which is complete with impressive animatronic goblins hard at work. Then, you're ushered down into the depths of the bank to meet with Bill Weasley for your tour. The queue is a lot of fun, even though some of the effects in Weasley's office aren't incredibly convincing. From here, board one of 12 passenger cars for your "tour," which quickly turns into an escape from the Dark Lord and his accomplice Bellatrix Lestrange. This attraction is a little tamer than Forbidden Journey, so young kids may fare better here.

Outdoor Shows in Diagon Alley

Running throughout the day are two different shows onstage by Carkitt Market. The first features the jazzy musical stylings of Celestina Warbeck and the Banshees, who, fans will remember, was Molly Weasley's favorite musician. The second show features two stories told with puppets from *The Tales of Beedle the Bard*: "The Fountain of Fair Fortune" and fan favorite "The Tale of the Three Brothers."

Dining and Shopping in Diagon Alley

When it's time for some food, head to the famous Leaky Cauldron. This is Diagon Alley's main dining experience, aside from food available at vendor carts and treats at Florean Fortescue's Ice-Cream Parlour. Here again, The Leaky Cauldron provides a true Harry Potter experience in ambience as well as menu. American-style meals are nowhere to be found inside; instead, you'll choose from a variety of British-style dishes, such as fish and chips; cottage pie (beef and vegetables under mashed potatoes); and beef, lamb, and Guinness stew are offered. To many parents' relief, the kids' menu does include macaroni and cheese (phew).

Also within Diagon Alley is Florean Fortescue's Ice-Cream Parlour. In the morning, this is a good spot to grab a quick continental breakfast and pastries. Later on, it's hard to resist stopping in for some unique ice cream flavors, such as chocolate chili,

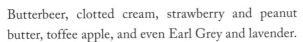

Butterbeer, clotted cream, strawberry and peanut butter, toffee apple, and even Earl Grey and lavender.

If you're thirsty, grab a beverage at the indoor pub, The Fountain of Fair Fortune, or the outdoor stand, The Hopping Pot. There are also street vendors offering quick-service options such as Eternelle's Elixir of Refreshment.

Shopping in Diagon Alley feels like an attraction all its own. True Harry Potter fans can spend hours perusing these shops for treasures. The many, many shopping options in Diagon Alley include Ollivanders, Weasleys' Wizard Wheezes, Madam Malkin's Robes for All Occasions, Magical Menagerie, Scribbulus Writing Implements, Wiseacre's Wizarding Equipment, Quality Quidditch Supplies, Borgin and Burkes, and Wands by Gregorovitch.

Ollivanders, as more thoroughly explained earlier in this chapter, is the place to get your wizardly wand.

Love a good magical joke? Head on over to Weasleys' Wizard Wheezes to pick up items such as Skiving

Snackboxes, U-No-Poo, Pygmy Puffs, Extendable Ears, Chinese Fortune Sticks, Bing Bong ginger snaps, and much, much more. Even if you aren't planning to purchase anything, this shop is worth a stop just to take in the props on the second floor and the fireworks that explode above you.

Madam Malkin's Robes for All Occasions sells beautiful robes and Hogwarts merchandise, including backpacks, scarves, and sweaters, a variety of stylish hats, and Gryffindor polo shirts.

The Magical Menagerie is where you can find plenty of plush and toy versions of your favorite magical Harry Potter creatures, such as Buckbeak, Scabbers, Fluffy, and Crookshanks, plus a variety of owls, cats, and rats.

Scribbulus Writing Implements provides all the writing materials a Hogwarts student needs, including feather quills, journals, postcards, parchment paper, glass ink wells, and more.

Wiseacre's Wizarding Equipment is located at the exit of Harry Potter and the Escape from Gringotts attraction. This store is filled with an assortment of binoculars, crystal balls, compasses, telescopes, magnifying glasses, hour glasses, and other wizardly equipment, along with a wide array of Harry Potter apparel.

Quality Quidditch Supplies is the perfect place for folks needing anything Quidditch-related, including Bludger bats, Golden Snitches, and Quaffles.

If you stroll down the more sinister Knockturn Alley, you can step into the world of dark magic inside the infamous Borgin and Burkes. You'll see eerie Death Eater masks, robes, and skulls, as well as apparel, collectibles, and jewelry.

If you'd rather not fight the crowds in Ollivanders you can visit the other, slightly darker, wand store: Wands by Gregorovitch. Just like in the Harry Potter series, you may not find the same friendly service offered at Ollivanders here.

GRIMMAULD PLACE, LONDON

If you pause a moment at 12 Grimmauld Place, which is Sirius Black's residence, watch the window above the door. Every few minutes, the curtain is pulled back and you'll catch a glimpse of Kreacher, the house-elf.

FASHION ADVICE

Would you like a magical opinion on your outfit while inside Madame Malkin's Robes for All Occasions shop? Simply stand in front of the large mirror and wait for a response. Warning: you won't always get a compliment.

IT'S A FACT

SHUTTERBUTTON'S MAGICAL PHOTO OPP

This shop may offer one of the coolest photographic keepsakes at the Universal Orlando Resort: magical moving photos—just like in the Harry Potter series …

- The studio will create 12 different moving pictures of you and your party inside The Wizarding World.

- You'll stand in front of a green screen and perform several actions, as directed by the staff. Then your video image is superimposed into Harry Potter scenes.

- Shutterbutton's provides a DVD with the videos to take home but the store plans to offer a picture frame displaying your magical photos as well.

IT'S A FACT

THE LEAKY CAULDRON

Did you notice that the cauldron on the Leaky Cauldron's sign in Diagon Alley actually leaks? Pause for a moment by the entrance to take a peek at this cool little detail.

Also worth a look at the Leaky Cauldron is the discreet, (non-functioning) door on the London facade between the bookshop and record shop. It's designed to be easy to miss, but the sign will tell you it's the entrance to the Leaky Cauldron—just like in the books.

SHH... IT'S A SECRET

ORLANDO FLORIDA

HARRY POTTER AND THE ESCAPE FROM GRINGOTTS

If you've got keen ears for recognizing voices, you may notice that Harry and Hermione's voices inside this attraction sound a little different. That's because the original actors Daniel Radcliffe and Emma Watson did not participate in this production; other actors impersonated them instead.

WHY IS OLLIVANDERS IN HOGSMEADE *AND* DIAGON ALLEY?

With J.K. Rowling's approval, Universal included Ollivanders in Hogsmeade because it was the original, and possibly only, Harry Potter area that was to be built. The resort hadn't yet confirmed plans for Diagon Alley. So the first shop opened in Hogsmeade, and a second shop opened in Diagon Alley. This is why Ollivanders wizardly workers at both shops will occasionally joke that their location is "the original."

IT'S A FACT

HARRY POTTER AND THE ESCAPE FROM GRINGOTTS

If you're wondering how Universal created the ride track for Harry Potter and the Escape from Gringotts, it's actually a 3-D multidimensional, multisensory coaster ride equipped with several motion bases along the way. This specialized ride track allowed Universal to make illusions, such as the feeling you're falling, seem very real. These tricks are similar to those used in The Amazing Adventures of Spider-Man attraction.

A CALL FROM THE MINISTRY

Every small detail you see in The Wizarding World of Harry Potter – Diagon Alley is there for a reason. For example, when you pass by the innocent-looking red phone booths in London's King's Cross Station outside Diagon Alley, stop inside and dial M-A-G-I-C. You'll hear a greeting from the Ministry of Magic.

Another fun fact: These phone booths were real, functioning booths from London, specially shipped to The Wizarding World of Harry Potter.

IT'S A
FACT

HARRY POTTER AND THE ESCAPE FROM GRINGOTTS

If you are impressed, as many people are, with the animatronic goblins in the Great Hall, try something fun: Ask one of them a question. They are designed to answer you.

QUALITY QUIDDITCH SUPPLIES

The Quidditch outfit and broom in the glass display cabinet at the back of the store was worn in one of the Harry Potter movies. There is no sign to explain, however, so it's unclear which actor donned what garb.

CHAPTER FOUR

UNIVERSAL CITYWALK

Universal CityWalk is a nighttime entertainment complex offering a multitude of dining options, bars, clubs, and live music. There you'll be able to enjoy performances by the Blue Man Group, play a round on Universal's Hollywood Drive-In Golf mini-golf course, or catch a movie at the massive AMC Universal Cineplex 20 with IMAX.

Dining options range from inexpensive fast food all the way to high-priced gourmet cuisine at establishments like the highly acclaimed Emeril's. There are so many food options at CityWalk, even the pickiest eaters should be able find their idea of dining nirvana.

There is also an array of clubs, bars, and live shows to explore, offering entertainment from reggae, to rock, to the Blue Man Group's unique percussion performances. Add the outdoor recreation and movie options and you'll know why CityWalk is a favorite nighttime destination for Orlando residents as well as Universal Orlando Resort guests. The area is buzzing almost every night. If you go, be aware that several clubs and even restaurants have a casual-chic dress code, so you may want to change clothes after your day at the park before heading over.

Originally focused on adult options for entertainment, CityWalk now appeals to families as well (the addition of mini-golf and movies helps).

What's especially nice about CityWalk is its close proximity to the parks and on-site hotels. Shuttles run back and forth late into the night to Universal's on-site hotels. You can enjoy a full evening of dinner and entertainment and still get back to your resort easily. This is a great destination to visit after you're done with the amusment parks, especially if you're not excited about the dining and entertainment options your hotel offers. Some of the more popular restaurants suggest a reservation, so be sure to plan ahead if your heart is set on a specific dining destination.

Dining in CityWalk

Antojitos Authentic Mexican Food is a newer addition that opened in 2014. The menu offers standard Mexican dishes such as enchiladas and chimichangas as well as new dishes to try like Mar Y Tierra Stew. Everything is made from scratch, including the guacamole made right at your table (though it's a little pricey).

Bob Marley – A Tribute to Freedom offers a chance to sit inside a replica of Bob Marley's Kingston home. Designed and created with the help of Bob Marley's widow, Rita, this restaurant features artifacts and photos that were donated by the Marley family, plus live reggae music performances. The menu is, of course, Jamaican-inspired, including dishes such as oxtail stew and Jamaican curry-marinated grilled chicken breast.

The Bubba Gump Shrimp Co. is a family restaurant specializing in, you guessed it, shrimp. You'll have other options here as well, including baby back ribs. Fans of the *Forrest Gump* movie will especially

enjoy this eatery; pause in front of the restaurant for a cute photo opp by stepping into plaster casts of Forrest's running shoes.

The Cowfish Sushi Burger Bar offers a somewhat unique combination of upscale burgers, sushi, hand-spun milkshakes, and salads. The menu includes items like the Jalapeño Popper Show-Stopper burger, the Big Squeal burger, sashimi, nigiri, and classic makimono. The restaurant states that ingredients are fresh and never frozen, and desserts are homemade.

Emeril's Restaurant Orlando is considered City-Walk's premier fine dining spot. It presents sophis-ticated Creole-based gourmet food and diners will enjoy watching the staff work in the open kitchen. Emeril's boasts a lovely atmosphere that includes a 12,000-bottle wine gallery in climate-controlled cases and even a cigar bar with a wall-sized humidor. At Emeril's, you're sure to have a memorable evening, but take note that this is one of the most expensive options in CityWalk.

Hard Rock Cafe Orlando is home to rock 'n' roll and American cuisine. This is the world's largest Hard Rock Cafe and houses the chain's biggest collection of rock 'n' roll memorabilia, including items from Elvis, The Beatles, KISS, Bob Dylan, and other musicians. The menu contains classic American entrées, including burgers, steak, and barbeque chicken.

Hot Dog Hall of Fame is a baseball and hotdog lover's paradise. This cute restaurant offers famous hotdogs designed to mimic the food from beloved baseball parks around the United States, or you can customize your own. A nice touch to the theming is the stadium seating as well as the artificial turf. Standard tables and chairs are also offered.

Jimmy Buffett's Margaritaville fits right into Orlando's CityWalk. The lovely indoor dining room features The Volcano Bar, Land Shark Bar, and 12 Volt Bar. The theme is inspired by Buffett's songs and the vibe of this restaurant is upbeat and laid-back all at once. Live bands play nightly, adding to

the restaurant's appeal. "Floribbean Cuisine" is featured here, a combination of Caribbean and Key West foods. The outside dining area named the Porch of Indecision offers the same menu and also features live music. Of course you'll also find some of the best margaritas around.

NBA City beckons basketball fans with its 33-foot-tall statue of NBA's "Logoman" and its display of hand-imprinted bronze basketballs of some famous NBA players. Inside you'll find a two-level restaurant and the NBA City Playground, where you can shoot some hoops yourself. The main floor actually possesses an NBA-regulation half-court, where folks can dine. Occasionally, NBA pros host clinics here. The food in NBA City is upscale American-style cuisine, with some simple entrées for the less adventurous as well.

Universal designed Pat O'Brien's in Orlando to be a near exact replica of the famous Pat O'Brien's in New Orleans, right down to the cracks in the walls.

Fans of this establishment will not be dissappointed. You'll find delicious—though casually presented—New Orleans dishes here as well as their famous Hurricane drink and entertaining dueling pianists that play throughout the evening. Aside from the bar area with piano players, there's also a balcony and patio for a more intimate experience.

Red Oven Pizza Bakery is a good choice if you're looking for a delicious but quick and inexpensive option at CityWalk. The pies are made while you watch and you can only order whole pies, no slices. The famous Red Oven is so hot, pizzas actually cook in 90 seconds. This may be your tastiest pizza option in the resort. Salads, soda, beer, and wine are available as well.

Vivo Italian Kitchen is the place for Italian fare at reasonable prices. This is a great family-friendly option, offering standard Italian dishes such as lasanga, fettucine carbonara, and pizza.

For quick service meals at CityWalk, you have several options. Bread Box handcrafted sandwiches

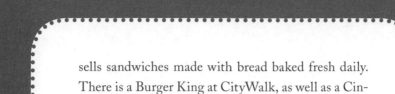

sells sandwiches made with bread baked fresh daily. There is a Burger King at CityWalk, as well as a Cinnabon serving up hard-to-resist cinnamon rolls.

If you're craving ice cream, drop in at Cold Stone Creamery for ice cream, shakes, and more. Fat Tuesday is ready to provide frozen drinks to beat the heat, and Fusion Bistro Sushi & Sake Bar offers Japanese favorites at this quick service stop.

Lone Palm Airport is a tiki bar located next to Jimmy Buffet's Margaritaville, serving drinks, along with nachos, hotdogs, wings, and more. Menchie's frozen yogurt has come to CityWalk, offering some delicious cool treats. Moe's Southwest Grill is your destination for a quick burrito, quesadilla, or salad, and Panda Express offers Chinese food, including orange chicken and Bejing beef. Lastly, Starbucks is here at CityWalk, as well as other locations in the Universal Orlando Resort.

Bars and Clubs in CityWalk

As mentioned earlier, Pat O'Brien's in Orlando is a near exact replica of the famous Pat O'Briens in New Orleans. This enjoyable, slightly rowdy bar offers the famous dueling pianos nightly. The pianists, who also sing, take requests from the crowd and can play almost anything. Part of the fun is seeing what song comes next and how much the crowd may end up singing along. Check out their famous Hurricane drinks, but be warned: they pack a punch.

CityWalk's Rising Star is Universal Orlando Resort's version of a karaoke club on steroids. Instead of the standard DJ and prerecorded library of backup tracks, you'll be fronting a full band of professional musicians, complete with backup singers. (Sunday and Monday nights only offer the backup singers as the rest of the musicians have the night off. On those nights, the music tracks are pre-recorded.) A Rising Star host keeps things moving along throughout the evening. The club opens at 8:00 P.M., and the band

starts playing at about 9:00 P.M. Tip: If you want a chance to sing, be sure to put your request in as early as possible. The host can't always get to everyone.

The Red Coconut Club at CityWalk is known for a cool, retro-chic '50s South Beach-meets-Las Vegas design. The music is centered mostly around Top 40 hits from the 1980s, played either by a DJ or band. There are three different bars inside along with an outdoor patio. Some of the delightful details here include bongo benches at the bar, a "swimming pool" dance floor, and the availability of VIP tables. Remember the dress code at the Red Coconut Club is casual-chic so your amusement park attire may need changing.

Dance club "the groove" is CityWalk's answer to a big city multi-floor nightclub but without the high fashion dress code. (The dress code here is casual-chic.) The groove's architectural style is designed to create the illusion of a century-old theater that is in multiple stages of repair, though the high-tech lighting, massive wall of video screens, and fog effects tend to distract from this intention. The dance floor is usually jumping to the sounds of a DJ and, on Friday evenings, local favorite DJ ET from radio station 102 JAMZ is on deck. When you're ready to take it down a notch, the groove offers three lounge rooms and a balcony for a quieter setting.

The original Bourbon Street drink spot, Fat Tuesday, is a walk-up bar serving a variety of frozen drinks, including margaritas, the famous 190 Octane, mudslides, the Eye Candy, and more.

As mentioned earlier, during the day Bob Marley – A Tribute to Freedom serves up some terrifically fun Jamaican cuisine, but after 9:00 P.M. each night, you'll catch some memorable live entertainment from a reggae band or DJ.

One would expect to find live music and entertainment at Jimmy Buffet's Margaritaville and sure enough there's plenty to be found. Inside, you can enjoy the house band while you get drinks at the cool Volcano Bar, or casually hang out on the Porch of

Indecision listening to a live guitarist belt out some tunes. Of course, the margaritas will be flowing in either location.

Live Music and Shows in CityWalk

If you're looking for something other than dining and clubbing at CityWalk, there are also plenty of options for live concerts and shows. The Hard Rock Live provides an ever-changing list of entertainment, including musical performances and famous comedians. If you want something completely unique, and family friendly, spend an evening with the Blue Man Group.

The Hard Rock Live is the first live performance venue that was built by the Hard Rock. The building's facade is modelled like a historic coliseum. Inside the "Coliseum of Rock 'n' Roll," you'll find a classic concert venue equipped with state-of-the-art sound, lighting, and video equipment. This facility holds a maximum of 3,000 people and hosts musical acts and comedians, and even dance and cheerleading competitions. Because the venue is on the smaller side, you won't see a contant stream of Platinum-selling artists here, but the shows will certainly rock and the performers usually have a great following. Previous performers at the Hard Rock Live have included Velvet Revolver, Beck, Nelly, Jewel, 311, Melissa Etheridge, Slayer, Wanda Sykes, and Howie Mandel.

Looking for something completely different? The Blue Man Group show, now a national phenomenon, started in New York simply as a very eccentric stage show featuring three men covered in blue. These shows are now found all around the country, offering different variations of the original, but are careful not to stray far from its origins. You've never seen anything quite like this show before; its filled with offbeat humor, funny tricks, and extremely talented musicianship brought forth on many unique instruments. This three-man

crew is backed by a band in an upper level as well. This is a show the whole family can enjoy (though it isn't recommended for kids under four).

Other Entertainment in CityWalk

Last but not least, Universal has installed two classic forms of American entertainment, especially—but not exclusively—geared toward families. CityWalk now offers the large AMC Universal Cineplex 20 with IMAX and the Hollywood Drive-In Golf mini-golf center.

The massive AMC Cineplex 20 with IMAX shows the current offering of major movies and includes an IMAX option as well as 3D. You'll find an expected array of movie-style snacks available at the concession stand, along with a selection of beer and wine.

Universal's Hollywood Drive-In Golf opened in 2012, offering another entertaining evening option at CityWalk for families. There are two 18-hole courses here, each designed to have the feel of the drive-in movies of the 1950s. One course, Invaders from Planet Putt, has a '50 sci-fi theme, while the second is a silly, haunted-themed course called "The Haunting of Ghostly Greens." These courses follow a "landscape" design rather than an "adventure" design, meaning the holes are not meant to be highly challenging. Theming here is cute and silly, which certainly provides for an entertaining family activity. LED neon edge lighting makes it especially enjoyable at night.

Shopping in CityWalk

Shopping isn't the main focus at CityWalk, but there are a few stores, including national chains, sprinkled into the area. You'll have your choice of The Universal Studios Store, which offers standard Universal Orlando Resort merchandise; Element, specializing in skateboards and related items; Fossil for watches and more; Fresh Produce and The Island Clothing Company for apparel; plus The Quiet Flight Surf Shop and the Hart & Huntington Tattoo Company.

TACTICAL **TIPS**

WHERE TO REVIEW MENUS

If you arrive at CityWalk and aren't sure where to eat, you can check out all the restaurant menus at once by stopping at the Dining Reservations and CityWalk Information window. They even have the restaurants' gluten-free menus on hand.

PRIORITY SEATING FOR ON-SITE HOTEL GUESTS

If you're staying at an on-site hotel (excluding the value-priced Cabana Bay Beach Hotel), you may get priority seating for dinner at CityWalk. Not all restaurants participate, but it's certainly worth making an inquiry. Your hotel can give you a list of which restaurants offer this nice perk.

HARD ROCK CAFE: VIBE TOUR

You can get a free "Vibe" tour at the Hard Rock café, where you'll get to see amazing rock 'n' roll memorabilia in rooms most guests never enter and hear all about the history of the Hard Rock. You'll even get to step inside "The Attic," which is where many artists hang out backstage after a performance. Rock fans will never forget their chance to take this tour, which most people don't even know about. Remarkable items you'll see include John Lennon and Yoko Ono's marriage certificate, a chair in which John Lennon wrote many of his famous songs, and a wall with seemingly countless signatures and comments from visiting artists.

TACTICAL **TIPS**

PARKING AT CITYWALK

Parking for CityWalk is free to Florida residents after 6:00 P.M. Proof of residency is required.

HOLLYWOOD DRIVE-IN GOLF

Did you know that, aside from the traditional scorecard and pencil available at Hollywood Drive-In Golf you can use a smart phone app?

Check out the Hollywood Drive-In Golf Scorecard App, which allows you to keep score for your party electronically. You can save your scores to your phone at the end of your game, in case you want proof for your bragging rights.

IT'S A FACT

BLUE MAN GROUP

If you have a student ID, you might be able to purchase discount tickets (up to two) the day of the show. Present your ID at the office.

If you purchase tickets to see Blue Man Group, you may be able to get same-day priority seating at CityWalk restaurants and free admission to clubs such as Rising Star as well. Present your ticket stub to the host at the entrance and ask if they participate.

Also note: U.S. Armed Forces members can buy discount tickets the day of the show. See your MWR, ITT, and ITR offices for details and to purchase tickets.

TACTICAL **TIP**

BLUE MAN GROUP

If you have a student ID, you might be able to purchase discount tickets (up to two) the day of the show. Present your ID at the office.

If you purchase tickets to see Blue Man Group, you may be able to get same-day priority seating at CityWalk restaurants and free admission to clubs such as Rising Star as well. Present your ticket stub to the host at the entrance and ask if they participate.

Also note: U.S. Armed Forces members can buy discount tickets the day of the show. See your MWR, ITT, and ITR offices for details and to purchase tickets.

CHAPTER FIVE

HOTELS AND WET 'N WILD WATERPARK

WHAT WOULD A POPULAR VACATION resort be without on-site hotel options? Universal Orlando Resort currently has four on-site hotels. You have three luxury choices: Hard Rock Hotel, Loews Portofino Bay Hotel, and Loews Royal Pacific Resort. The value-priced Cabana Bay Beach Resort opened in 2014. Expanding your choices, Universal is currently building Loews Sapphire Falls Resort, which is scheduled to open in 2016. All hotels are close to the two Universal amusement parks and CityWalk, and Universal wisely offers several exclusive park and CityWalk perks for on-site hotel guests.

Though it isn't officially part of the resort, next door is Universal-owned Wet 'n Wild Waterpark. Universal offers packages that include tickets to Wet 'n Wild, if you so desire.

Many visitors simply book a shuttle to visit Universal Orlando Resort while they are vacationing at Walt Disney World, but Universal offers award-winning resorts of its own, with many perks to entice you. It's worth considering even a partial stay at one of Univeral's on-site resorts. The Universal accommodations are not only convenient, but also a good value. It's certainly worth comparision shopping before you book your trip.

Wet 'n Wild Waterpark may be the perfect addition to a stay at the Universal Orlando Resort if the weather is hot and you're ready to put in some real water time. Shuttles run back and forth between Wet 'n Wild and the on-site hotels so it isn't difficult to schedule a day here.

TACTICAL **TIPS**

HOTEL PERK: UNLIMITED EXPRESS PASS

Guests at any of Universal's luxury hotels (this does not include the value-priced Cabana Bay) receive a free Unlimited Express Pass for each day of their stay. (Park ticket purchase is required.) This is a big plus because it allows you to access shorter, Express Pass lines all day long.

HOTEL PERK: FREE SHUTTLES TO THEME PARKS AND CITYWALK

All of Universal's on-site resorts offer free shuttle service to its theme parks as well as CityWalk. The three luxury hotels offer a cool water taxi option. Shuttles from CityWalk run as late as 2:00 A.M.

TACTICAL **TIPS**

HOTEL PERK: PRIORITY SEATING AT SELECT RESTAURANTS

If you're staying at one of Universal's luxury resorts (this excludes Cabana Bay), you can obtain priority seating at certain restaurants within the resort. These include Mythos, Lombard's Seafood Grille, Jimmy Buffett's Margaritaville Cafe, Hard Rock Cafe, Emeril's, and Bob Marley – A Tribute to Freedom.

HOTEL PERK: TRANSPORTATION TO WET 'N WILD, SEAWORLD, AND AQUATICA

Although these destinations are not part of Universal Orlando Resort, there are free, scheduled transportation buses offered to these locations from Universal's on-site hotels.

Hotels & Water Park

TACTICAL **TIP**

HOTEL PERK: KIDS CLUBS

If your family is staying at one of Universal's on-site hotels, you may decide to take advantage of the adult-supervised kids clubs (ages 4 to 14) so the grown-ups can get a night out alone. There are three clubs here, but usually only one is open at a time. They are open evening hours although expanded hours are offered during certain times of the year.

Any guest of Universal's on-site hotels has access to the club that's operating at that time. Loews Portofino Bay Hotel houses Campo Portofino, Hard Rock Hotel runs Camp Lil' Rock, and Loews Royal Pacific Resort offers The Mariner's Club. Cabana Bay guests also have access to these clubs. There is a fee per child for use of the club. Reservations are recommended.

TACTICAL **TIP**

LOEWS LOVES KIDS PROGRAM

Loews luxury on-site hotels offer a variety of kid perks through its Loews Loves Kids Program, including…

- A welcome gift to kids under 10.

- The "Kids Closet" loans items—such as toys, books, strollers, nightlights, outlet protectors, and baby bathtubs—to make your stay easier.

- Child-proof kits for families traveling with children under four.

- The Loews Kids Club program, offering adult-supervised childcare (Cabana Bay guests also have access to this).

- Baby-sitting.

Hotels & Water Park

TACTICAL **TIP**

PETS ARE WELCOME, BUT NOT EVERYWHERE

Universal's three luxury hotels, Portofino Bay Hotel, Hard Rock Hotel, and Royal Pacific Resort are pet-friendly. These hotels offer a limited number of pet-friendly rooms, which are separate from the other rooms at the hotel so guests without pets are not exposed to any extra noise or dander.

Each of these pet-friendly hotels offers a map of areas where you are free to walk your pet. Cleaning staff are not allowed into a room with a pet unless you are present, so the hotel will set up a special time when the room can be cleaned. Note: There is an extra cleaning fee if you bring your pet.

At these Universal luxury hotels, you can even order special meals from gourmet pet room-service menus and you can obtain specialized bedding, leashes, litter boxes (and litter), pet placemats, water bowls, treats, catnip, and much more.

Cabana Bay Beach Resort does not allow pets.

TACTICAL **TIPS**

START YOUR DAY THE UNIVERSAL WAY

Guests of any on-site Universal hotel can schedule a character wake-up call. You can choose between several Universal characters and hear a fun wake-up message in the morning.

UNIVERSAL'S "DIVE-IN" MOVIES

Each of Universal's on-site hotels offer Dive-In movie events, where you and your family can watch family favorites and blockbuster movies on a big screen in the hotel's pool area. It's an enjoyable and relaxing way to spend the evening after an exciting day at the park.

CABANA BAY BEACH RESORT

Cabana Bay Beach Resort, which opened in 2014, is Universal's answer to the demand for a value-priced resort. This cleverly designed, retro 1950s and 1960s beach-themed hotel is entertaining, colorful, and quirky. Each of its buildings are named after classic hotels from the era that inspired the resort's design, including the Castaway and Thunderbird. You and your family will feel like you're stepping back in time everywhere you look, from the rooms' vintage décor to the hallway lighting and rugs. There are even classic '50s and '60s mint-condition cars at the entrance.

Room prices are a good value, especially since this is a newer facility. Though the design is retro, you'll find modern amenities in the 1,800 rooms, such as USB in-wall charging units, free wi-fi, and a 40-inch flat-screen TV with cable. Family suites are equipped with kitchenettes.

Though this is Universal's value-priced hotel, facilities at the Cabana Bay Beach Resort won't leave guests disappointed. There are two zero-entry pools surrounded by a sandy beach and an abundance of lounge chairs. Private, simply designed cabanas are available for rent daily. One pool offers a 100-foot waterslide and Cabana Bay also boasts Universal's first lazy river. Multiple activities are offered through-out the day and evenings, including ping-pong, volleyball, hula hoop contests, and "Dive-In" outdoor movie nights. There's even a live band or DJ playing tunes to keep things lively. Cabana Bay also houses a 10-lane bowling alley, Galaxy Bowl, and the Game-O-Rama high-tech arcade.

Dining at Cabana Bay Beach Resort

The Bayliner Food Court is a cafeteria-style eatery offering sandwiches, pizza, pasta, and hotdogs. Breakfast options include eggs, pancakes, fruit, pastry, waffles, yogurt, and more. There's plenty of seating here, either inside or outside by the pool.

There's also a Starbucks Coffee next to the Bayliner Food Court.

Inside the Galaxy Bowl is a smaller full-service dining area where you can order burgers, sandwiches, pizza, and more.

For drinks, you can visit a variety of bars, including one across from the check-in desk in the lobby called Swizzle, or an outside pool bar called Atomic Tonic.

TACTICAL **TIPS**

NO UNLIMITED EXPRESS PASSES

Keep in mind that, unlike Universal's luxury hotels, the value-priced Cabana Bay Beach Resort does not provide complimentary unlimited Express Passes. So though you are getting a great price on the room, the absence of this big perk is something to consider.

DOWN THE LAZY RIVER

Cabana Bay Beach Resort's lazy river is accessible to any of its guests, but there is a "hidden" fee. You need to purchase the tube you ride in. (You can keep the tube.) Budget-conscious travelers may want to purchase less expensive tubes elsewhere and bring them along.

TACTICAL **TIP**

CABANA BAY PERK: EARLY ADMISSION TO THE WIZARDING WORLD

If you have purchased park tickets while staying at the Cabana Bay Beach Resort, you'll have the opportunity to enter The Wizarding World of Harry Potter one hour early. (Whether your family can get up and be at the park for 8:00 A.M. is for you to decide.) All of Universal's on-site hotels offer this perk.

LOEWS ROYAL PACIFIC HOTEL

Visit the exotic South Seas during your stay in Orlando by booking a room at the Loews Royal Pacific Hotel. This award-winning hotel sits on 53 acres typified by lush foliage, including bamboo trees, an orchid court, and palm trees. The centerpiece of Loews Royal Pacific Hotel is the lovely 12,000-square-foot lagoon-style pool. This area features a sand beach, the Royal Bali Sea children's interactive water-play area, two hot tubs, and private cabanas available for rent. Cabana amenities include a ceiling fan, fridge stocked with water and soda, and TV. Activities are available in the pool area as well, including volleyball, ping-pong, pool basketball, and arts and crafts. There is also the Dive-In outdoor movie night. The not-to-miss event at the Loews Royal Pacific Hotel is the Wantilan Luau, featuring a Polynesian buffet.

The Loews Royal Pacific Hotel houses approximately 750 rooms. Each room is outfitted with a 32-inch flat-panel TV, an iHome clock radio with iPod docking station, a Keurig coffeemaker with Emeril's coffee, and Lather skin-care products. Most rooms have a separate bath and vanity area. Complimentary high-speed wireless access is available in public areas of the hotel, but a fee is required for room access.

Other amenities at the Loews Royal Pacific Hotel include the Gymnasium (a 5,000-square-foot fitness center), the Mariner's Club supervised kids' camp for children, ages 4 to 14, a game room arcade, access to the Mandara Spa (located at Loews Portofino Bay Hotel), jogging paths, gift shops, and more. The Mandara Spa offers an array of spa treatments based on Balinese traditions such as the Mandara Four Hand Massage, Mandara Balinese Body Polish, and Mandara Hot Stone Massage.

Dining at Loews Royal Pacific Hotel

There are several dining options at Loews Royal Pacific Hotel, including Islands Dining Room, Emeril's Tchoup Chop, Jake's American Bar, the Bula Bar & Grille, Orchid Court Lounge, Orchid Court Sushi Bar, and the Wantilan Luau.

The Islands Dining Room is the hotel's main dining room, serving Pan Asian cuisine with a twist. Breakfast includes standard American favorites along with some Polynesian-influenced specialties. Kids may enjoy the children's dining room, which is equipped with youth-sized tables and chairs, a TV playing cartoons, and a Balinese-style play area. The Islands Dining Room also hosts Universal Orlando character dining on select nights.

Emeril's Tchoup Chop is one of the star restaurants for on-site hotel dining at Universal. Celebrity chef Emeril Lagasse has created a bold and adventurous

menu of exotic Pacific Seas dishes. The ambience matches the menu with stunning decor that creates a memorable evening. Reservations are suggested.

Jake's American Bar—themed around a fictional 1930s-era, island-hopping pilot named Jake McNally—is a favorite spot for casual dining. You'll find American-style dining options, including the Bomber Bacon Burger, fish and chips, crab cake sandwiches, pork chops, and steak. If you're a beer lover, there's a four-course beer dinner. Jake's also hosts a Universal character breakfast on select Sundays. Reservations are recommended.

If you'd like a quick meal so you can get an early start, grab a continental breakfast every morning at the Orchid Court Lounge. The room is decorated with an array of orchids and hand-carved Balinese furniture. You can also find cocktails, lunch, and dinner here, including salads, burgers, and wraps.

The Orchid Court Sushi Bar offers another chance to experience South Pacific-inspired dining, with an extensive sushi and sashimi menu along with South Seas cocktails and Asian-inspired desserts.

The Bula Bar & Grille is a poolside food option offering a variety of beers and cocktails and delicious sandwiches, nachos, quesadillas, burgers, and salads. If you're looking for a casual, less expensive option with good food, this may be your ticket.

Hosted on most Saturday evenings, the very popular Wantilan Luau offers guests a chance to experience a traditional Hawaiian luau. Enjoy an all-you-can-eat Polynesian buffet while live Hawaiian music swirls around you and hula dancers put on an exciting show. Reservations are recommended.

IT'S A FACT

EMERIL'S TCHOUP CHOP RESTAURANT

Ever wonder how Emeril's Tchoup Chop restaurant got its interesting name? Pronounced "chop-chop," this upscale restaurant was named after the street where Emeril Lagasse's flagship restaurant resides in New Orleans: Tchoupitoulas Street.

Hotels & Water Park

HARD ROCK HOTEL

If you stay at the award-winning Hard Rock Hotel, it's likely you'll never forget it. Music-lovers will be enthralled with the rock 'n' roll memorabilia (worth more than a cool $1 million) that decorates this hip, artistic yet casual hotel. Elegance meets rock 'n' roll here, and the intention is to let you feel what it's like to live like a rock star.

The Hard Rock Hotel houses approximately 650 rooms, with standard rooms providing 375 to 400 square feet of living space and suites ranging from 650 to 2,375 square feet. In-room amenities include a 32-inch flat screen TV, a Keurig coffee-maker with assorted coffees and teas, an iHome clock radio with iPod docking station, separate bath and vanity area, and evening turndown service upon request. Wireless high-speed Internet is available in your room for a fee.

The Hard Rock Hotel boasts some great amenities, such as a 12,000-square-foot pool, access to the Mandara Spa (located at Loews Portofino Bay Hotel), a fitness center, concerts, the Camp Lil' Rock kids club (see the beginning of this chapter for additional information), jogging paths, and more. Just strolling around the building and gazing at the seemingly endless rock memorabilia displayed here could be a favorite activity for music fans.

The Hard Rock Hotel's centerpiece is the lovely sand beach pool that features an underwater stereo sound system, an interactive children's water-play area, a 260-foot waterslide, and poolside activities including a sand volleyball court, ping-pong, two hot tubs, hula-hoop contests, pool basketball, Dive-In movies, and concerts on select evenings. Private cabanas are available for rent as well, and they include an HD plasma TV, ceiling fan, soda- and water-stocked fridge, and wireless Internet.

Guests of the Hard Rock Hotel have access to services at the nearby Mandara Spa, located in Loews Portofino Bay Hotel. The Mandara Spa offers an array of spa treatments based on Balinese traditions such as the Mandara Four Hand Massage, Mandara Balinese Body Polish, and Mandara Hot Stone Massage. The Workout Room fitness center houses cardio-fitness and circuit-training equipment, along with steam and sauna rooms. The Fitness Room charges an entry fee.

Dining at the Hard Rock Hotel

The Hard Rock Hotel is certainly not lacking in dining options, including some family-friendly destinations as well as stylish places to enjoy a cocktail.

The famous Palm Restaurant originated in Manhattan and now has come to Orlando with its installation at the Hard Rock. Known for incredible steaks and lobster, the restaurant also offers other classic American fare and traditional Italian entrées. This is a pricey dining experience, so be prepared. Reservations are suggested.

The Kitchen is a family-friendly, casual dining option offering American cuisine in an open restaurant atmosphere that's designed to feel like the kitchen in a celebrity's mansion. Breakfast, lunch, and dinner are served. The Kitchen houses The Kids Crib, which is a special area for children with kid-sized tables and chairs, beanbag chairs, and a TV showing cartoons.

This is where you can catch the Hard Rock Hotel's character dining opportunity on select nights. The Kitchen also hosts Kids Can Cook Too! nights, as well as performances by magicians, balloon artists, and more. Occasionally, a visiting artist will perform a cooking demonstration at the Chef's Table.

If you're spending some time poolside, grab some refreshing drinks or snacks at the Beachclub. Some of the fun rock-themed drinks include the Sweet Home Alabama, Blue Suede Shoes, and the Raspberry Beret.

One of the coolest bars around is the artistic Velvet Bar. Elaborately styled with zany zebra chairs and memorabilia on the walls, this is a great place to hang out for drinks before dinner or afterwards.

If you're in search of a frozen treat, head to Emack & Bolio's Marketplace for ice cream, sorbets, and frozen yogurts. Fun music-inspired flavors include Bye Bye Miss American Mud Pie and Jumping Jack Grasshopper Pie.

Hard Rock Hotel Music Entertainment

It only makes sense that the Hard Rock Hotel would include the opportunity to hear some great A-list music. On the last Thursday of each month (with the exception of November and December) the Velvet Bar hosts the Velvet Sessions. Combining a more intimate performance experience with cocktails and finger food, the Velvet Sessions can be a musical highlight of your Orlando trip.

IT'S A FACT

HARD ROCK HOTEL "PICKS"

What is one of the most rockin' in-room amenities offered in all of the Universal Orlando Resort? The Hard Rock Hotel offers its unique Picks option to guests, where a guitar or bass guitar will be delivered to your room, complete with an amp and headphones (because other guests may not appreciate the rockin' noise). You can select from a list of 20 different Fender guitars and basses.

There is no charge for this cool way to unwind in your room. You do, however, need to provide a credit card deposit of $1,000, in case you can't part with your new toys.

TACTICAL **TIP**

COOL CABANA UPGRADE

If you decide to rent a private cabana by the pool at the Hard Rock Hotel, you can upgrade your experience by selecting a special cabana themed to be like The Beatles' "Yellow Submarine" or Stevie Wonder's "Musiquarium."

Hotels & Water Park

IT'S A
FACT

THE VELVET SESSIONS

Artists who have performed at the Hard Rock Hotel's Velvet Sessions include…

- The Romantics
- Foreigner
- The Tubes
- Vince Neil
- Joan Jett
- Eddie Money
- The Fixx
- Bret Michaels
- Blue Oyster Cult
- Modern English
- The Go-Go's

LOEWS PORTOFINO BAY HOTEL

The award-wining Loews Portofino Bay Hotel transports you to the picturesque travel destination of Portofino, Italy. The architecture here has been modeled to replicate this lovely seaside town, where you'll stroll along cobblestone streets and view Italian cypress trees. Although Portofino Bay Hotel is decidedly upscale and comes with a luxury price tag, make no mistake—this is a family-friendly (and pet-friendly) hotel.

The accommodations are styled with a sleek Mediterranean flair, and some are loaded with extras that one would expect from a luxury hotel. In-room amenities include a Keurig coffeemaker with Emeril's gourmet coffee, Lather skin-care products, 32-inch flat-screen TV, cotton signature bathrobes, and evening turndown service. In-Room wireless high-speed service is available for a fee. There are 750 rooms available at Loews Portofino Bay Hotel, including standard rooms that are approximately 450 square feet, and suites ranging from 650 to 3,215 square feet.

Other amenities at Loews Portofino Bay Hotel include three themed pools, the Mandara Spa and Fitness Center, game rooms, bocce ball courts, a kids club, jogging and walking paths, and the evening "Muscia della Notte" (Italian for "Music of the Night") performance in the hotel's Harbor Piazza.

The three pools are each designed with a specific focus in mind. The Beach Pool is a family-oriented pool that features a Roman aqueduct-style waterslide, a children's pool, poolside activities, and Universal's weekly outdoor Dine-In movies. Private cabanas are available for rent and include ceiling fans and a flat-panel TV. The Villa Pool is designed to offer more exclusivity, and upgraded amenities and lounge chairs. Cabanas are also available for rent here. The smaller, but very private, Hillside Pool on the east wing offers peace and quiet, away from all the activity.

The Mandara Spa and Fitness Center is a great place to unwind or get in your workout while at Universal Orlando Resort. The Spa offers an array of treatments based on Balinese traditions such as the Mandara Four Hand Massage, Mandara Balinese Body Polish, and Mandara Hot Stone Massage. The Fitness Center offers an array of workout equipment, including stair climbers, elliptical cross-trainers, steam and sauna rooms, treadmills, and more.

In the evening, gather in the hotel's Harbor Piazza to experience the Muscia della Notte. Performers create a blend of classic opera, romantic music, and even "popera," which is music intended to bridge the gap between popular music and opera.

Dining at Loews Portofino Bay Hotel

As you can imagine, you'll have several choices for Italian cuisine, along with a mix of American dining, at the Portofino Bay Hotel.

Enjoy traditional Italian family dining at Mama Della's Ristorante while strolling musicians add to the ambience. The menu features Old World favorites from Naples, Tuscany, and Piedmonte. Entrée choices include lasagna, fettuccine Alfredo, frutti di mare, and pesce spada alla griglia.

Bice Ristorante is part of a renowned chain of casual yet elegant Italian cuisine. This string of restaurants was started by Beatrice ("Bice" as friends called her) Ruggeri in 1926 and has expanded throughout the globe all the while being carefully overseen by the Ruggeri family. This is a high-priced Italian experience, and reservations are recommended. The menu offers Northern Italian cuisine,

including some classic Italian dishes and new favorites to discover.

Trattoria del Porto offers a friendly, casual dining option at the Portofino Bay Hotel. Breakfast is served daily, including a breakfast buffet on select mornings. Evening dining offers brasserie-style food, including mahi mahi, pancetta-wrapped meatloaf, burgers, and roasted chicken. There are child-sized chairs and tables here, along with bean-bag chairs, a play area, and a large-screen TV playing cartoons. This is where you can catch a Universal Orlando character dinner on select nights. Trattoria del Porto also offers Pasta Cucina ("Kitchen") on select evenings, where you can invent your own food creations from a selection of pastas, sauces, and other ingredients.

Stroll into Sal's Market Deli for a quick bite, including sandwiches, salads, and fresh-made pizza. Making pizza at Sal's is serious business, with home-made dough baked in an open oven while you watch.

(Gluten-free pizzas are available here as well.) You can also grab a glass of wine or beer at Sal's.

The Thirsty Fish is a nice spot to stop by for a glass of wine, a beer, a quick snack of hummus, or an antipasto plate. Outdoor seating is especially nice when the weather is good, and live jazz music can be enjoyed on select nights.

The Bar American is an upscale hotel lounge offering a wide selection of cocktails and drinks, as well as a small menu of items to munch on, including bianca flatbread, mussels, and turkey burgers.

If you're relaxing by the pool you can get a bite to eat at the super-casual Splendido Bar & Grill, which offers a large array of cocktails, (including frozen drinks) and food choices such as seafood chowder, chips and salsa, chicken tenders, pizza, salads, and sandwiches.

When you're ready for an Italian-style treat, head to Gelateria for homemade gelato, biscotti, espresso, and more. There's also Starbucks located in the Harbor Piazza.

IT'S A FACT

WHY PORTOFINO?

Can you guess who provided the inspiration to build this hotel themed around the travel destination of Portofino, Italy? It actually was acclaimed film producer Steven Spielberg who first suggested this theme to Universal while he was consulting with Universal during the design of Islands of Adventure's Jurassic Park.

WET 'N WILD WATERPARK

If it's a day of water fun you're looking for, take a trip to neighboring Wet 'n Wild Waterpark. Wet 'n Wild is not officially part of Universal Orlando Resort, but it is owned by Universal and you can obtain packages that include tickets to the park if you're staying at an on-site hotel. There are also scheduled shuttles that run to Wet 'n Wild from these hotels.

Wet 'n Wild is approximately 25 acres filled with watery entertainment. The park is mostly known for its multitude of multiperson attractions, allowing you and your party to experience the rides all together. There are a total of 15 attractions to be enjoyed here, ranging from Blastaway Beach, the children's waterplay area; to individual thrill rides such as the Aqua Drag Racer; group attractions like the Brain Wash; and activities like The Knee Ski. Here's a quick rundown of the current attractions at Wet 'n Wild.

Aqua Drag Racer

This is a four-lane race attraction featuring 350 feet of twisting, exciting track. The ride starts 65 feet above the ground to provide an adrenaline rush from the start of your adventure.

The Black Hole: The Next Generation

This space adventure incorporates lights and dynamic effects as you blast your way through this ride in a two person "hydra capsule" tube.

The Blast

Take a wild ride down a ruptured pipeline in this exciting multiperson flume ride.

Blastaway Beach

This sprawling one-acre family area opened in 2014 and offers a giant 60-foot-tall castle, two pools, 15 slides, and more than 160 interactive water features, including water cannons, soakers, jets, and waterfalls.

Bomb Bay

Do you have the courage to step inside this person-sized cylinder styled like a bomb, where the floor drops beneath you? You'll then explode straight down a heart-pumping 76-foot vertical drop. This is definitely for thrill seekers only.

Brain Wash

Riders may be hypnotized by the lights, sound, and video inside this six-story multiperson extreme tube ride, which features a 54-foot vertical drop into a 65-foot domed funnel.

Der Stuka

Inspired by the Junkers Ju-87 Stuka dive-bomber from World War II, Der Stuka gives you a chance to experience a "free fall" down a nearly vertical six-story speed slide.

Disco H2O

Enjoy a 1970s-themed multiperson flume ride inside this watery disco nightclub equipped with a sound system playing '70s hits, lights. There's even a disco ball or two.

The Flyer

The Flyer provides 450 feet of exciting banked curves on this four-passenger in-line toboggan adventure ride.

Lazy River

When it's time to slow down, catch a ride along the Lazy River that winds around the water park.

Mach 5

There are three different paths to choose from on this winding and twisting 1,700-foot flume ride.

The Storm

Designed to make you feel like you're inside a watery tornado, this ride drops riders through an elevated chute, where you'll spin just like a cyclone into a giant bowl.

The Surge

Swirl and twirl down this five story multipassenger tube ride featuring a track spanning nearly 600 feet of fun.

Surf Lagoon

Body surf the perfect wave in this 17,000-square-foot wave pool producing four-foot high waves.

Exciting Extras

Wet 'n Wild Waterpark also offers some extras along its Lake Sandy, including Knee Ski (kneeboarding), Wake Skating (knee skiing or wake skiing), or paddle boarding.

Dining at Wet 'n Wild

There are a variety of dining options in Wet 'n Wild, including Bubba's Fried Chicken and Ribs, Surf Grill, Manny's Pizza & Subs, and the Unlimited BBQ.

Hotels & Water Park

IT'S A
FACT

WET 'N WILD

Here are a few details you might not guess about Wet 'n Wild...

- Wet 'n Wild was the first "official" waterpark ever created. It was opened by the creator and founder of SeaWorld, George Millay, in 1977.

- Wet 'n Wild has more multiperson water attractions than any other waterpark in Orlando.

- When Aqua Drag Racer opened in 2014, it was the tallest and fastest ride of its kind in all of Florida.

ABOUT THE WRITER

LAURIE FLANNERY is a travel expert, writer, and parent to three energetic kids. She has contributed to several popular travel series and written for parenting, family travel, and music magazines. She lives in New England with her family.

Copyright Notices